Insect Physiology

INSECT PHYSIOLOGY

W. MORDUE

Professor, University of Aberdeen

G. J. GOLDSWORTHY

Reader, University of Hull

J. BRADY

Reader, Imperial College London

W. M. BLANEY

Senior Lecturer, Birkbeck College, London

BLACKWELL SCIENTIFIC PUBLICATIONS

OXFORD LONDON EDINBURGH
BOSTON MELBOURNE

© 1980 by Blackwell Scientific Publications
Editorial offices:
Osney Mead, Oxford, OX2 0EL
8 John Street, London WC1N 2ES
9 Forrest Road, Edinburgh, EH1 2QH
52 Beacon Street, Boston
    Massachusetts, 02108 USA
214 Berkeley Street, Carlton
    Victoria 3053, Australia

First published 1980

Set by DMB Services
Oxford, and
printed and bound in Great Britain by
Billing & Sons Ltd.
Guildford, Worcester and London

Distributed in USA and Canada by
Halsted Press, a Division of
John Wiley and Sons Inc
New York

British Library
Cataloguing in Publication Data

Insect physiology
    1. Insects - Physiology
    I. Mordue, W
    595.7′01   QL495
    ISBN 0-632-00385-5

Contents

Introduction

Insects are of incalculable importance to man. They are our major rivals for domination of this planet, and yet paradoxically they are also vital to our survival on it. On the one hand, they destroy our food—both before and after harvest—damage the wooden structure of our houses, and transmit our most devastating diseases. But on the other, they pollinate our crops, control many of our pests, and return much of our wastes to the soil. The impact of these effects is due mainly to the sheer numerical weight of insects, both as individuals (a colony of army ants may number 20 million and a swarm of locusts five times that), and as species (some 3 million).

In their evolution, insects are relatively ancient, having first appeared as Collembola in the Devonian (at roughly the same time as the first vertebrates), and as recognizable cockroaches, grasshoppers and dragonflies in the Carboniferous (at least 300 million years ago), thereafter ruling the air for 100 million years as the only flying animals. They have thus proved to be a phenomenally successful biological design which has survived unchanged in its basic winged form from a time that pre-dates the appearance of the first reptiles. A design, moreover, which has proved adaptable to almost every imaginable habitat, from arid deserts to freshwater lakes, and from volcanic springs at 80°C to arctic tundra at −20°C, with the only major unexploited niche being the open sea; and even that contains a few species.

What is it about this design that has made insects so successful? Is it the possession of a rigid, impermeable exoskeleton, the ability to fly, their high reproductive potential, or their small size? Or is it the adaptability of their behaviour, physiology and biochemistry to changing conditions? Probably it is all these things, and more. Physiologists study insects partly to answer these questions, to find out how insects work as biological machines, and partly to discover better means of controlling them when they are pests; they may, in addition, study them because they are convenient model systems for exploring more general physiological problems.

INSECTS AS MODELS

All animals, regardless of their level of organization, are faced with similar functional problems—respiration, water and ion balance, feeding and digestion, reproduction, locomotion, sensory perception, and so on. They have, however, often evolved different structural solutions to common problems. Compare, for example, the complex glomerular apparatus of vertebrate kidneys with the simple Malpighian tubules of insects (§ 2.3.1), or the respiratory circulatory system of vertebrates with the tracheae of insects (§ 1.1), or the totally different mechanics of insect and bird flight (§ 5.3.1). On the other hand, although the morphological and anatomical differences may be great, there are often underlying similarities of design and function at the cellular level (§ 1.3). For example, the major differences between the nervous or muscular systems of insects and vertebrates are to be found in the distribution of their excitable cells, rather than in fundamental dissimilarities in their mechanisms of action (Chapters 4 and 5).

Because insects are small by vertebrate standards, but their cells are of roughly the same size, insect organs contain less cells than their vertebrate equivalents, and their organization may thus be simpler. This is exploited by comparative physiologists as an aid to understanding general physiological problems. At the functional level, however, the simplicity may in some cases be deceptive, since the range of activities of any one insect cell may be greater than that of a comparable vertebrate cell, because the insect cell is less strongly differentiated. Nevertheless, insects do make ideal experimental animals: they are cheap to breed in large numbers, tolerant of operations, have an open blood system that makes transplantation experiments easy, and are so varied in form and habit that a species suitable for almost any particular physiological problem can usually be found.

THE CONTROL OF INSECT PESTS

The widespread and often inefficient use of insecticides such as DDT has resulted in the development and proliferation of strains of insects highly resistant to the chemicals used, and often in the unforeseen destruction of the pest's natural enemies. As a result, the pest not infrequently flourishes in even greater numbers than before. The need for more rational insecticide use, as well as for the development of alternative means of control is very evident. We need to know much more than we do at the moment about how insecticides act physiologically (§ 4.9) and about how they enter and are degraded in the insect's body—problems for which the study of insect physiology is vital. As for the development of alternatives to the DDT generation of insecticide control, some successes have already been achieved in the development of novel and more selective insecticides (§ 3.6) and artificial pheromones for disrupting mating behaviour (§ 6.6) or for more subtle forms of biological control. A deeper knowledge of insect physiology and behaviour is the key to the development of all such techniques.

INSECT PHYSIOLOGY AND THIS BOOK

As with any other animal, the insect's success in its environment depends on its ability to maintain its internal state within certain tolerable limits of pH, osmotic pressure, oxygenation, temperature, and so on. That is, it must maintain internal homeostasis. Being mainly terrestrial animals, insects possess two prime features which militate against their homeostasis: their small size and their rigid cuticle. Smallness is associated with a number of physiological problems due mainly to the fact that small animals have high surface to volume ratios (§ 7.1). The impermeability of the cuticle, while alleviating some of these problems, imposes difficulties of its own, especially for the uptake of materials from the environment (oxygen, water, food), for the removal of wastes (CO_2, water, excretions), and for the performance of behaviour. The insect's homeostatic problems, which are inevitably its physiological problems, are the subject of this book.

Knowledge of the physiology of insects has developed extensively over the last twenty years, and continues to develop as physiological technologies become more sophisticated. We have attempted to present an up to date and reasonably comprehensive account which emphasizes these advances while drawing attention to the limitations and limits of current research. The background of physiology required of the reader is minimal—about that expected of second year undergraduates—but a knowledge of the basic organization, morphology and diversity of insects is assumed. We believe that biochemistry and behaviour are integral parts of physiology, and we have included them as such—an approach not always adopted in undergraduate courses on insect physiology. A physiologist these days must be conversant with a wide array of disciplines, ranging from membrane biophysics, through biochemistry and cell biology, to the analysis of behaviour. We have tried to cover these fields in a comprehensive way at an introductory level, but inevitably in a short book we have had to be somewhat selective. We hope that nothing of substance has been omitted. Thus, whereas we have not provided a full reference list, key original papers are given throughout the text, and key titles for further reading are appended to each chapter. The enquiring student should receive a thorough introduction to the whole broad sweep of the subject if he follows these leads. We hope that he finds it an enjoyable experience.

Chapter 1
Energy Metabolism

1.1 SUPPLY OF OXYGEN TO THE TISSUES

Perhaps the major characteristic of metabolism in pterygote insects is their capacity for high rates of muscular activity under aerobic conditions. Thus, although the rate of respiration increases dramatically during flight, after flight has ceased the respiratory rate returns almost immediately to the pre-flight level; there is no build up of an oxygen debt. The rate of oxygen consumption in a flying blowfly may be 5 ml. min^{-1}. g^{-1} (the most intense respiration known to biologists)— some 30-50 times that of leg and heart muscle of a man at maximum activity. How is oxygen supplied to the tissues at such high rates?

Insect blood plays little or no part in the transport of respiratory gases. Instead, oxygen is carried directly to the tissues, and carbon dioxide escapes from them, by a system of internal tubes, the *tracheae*. These develop from invaginations of the epidermis and consist of tubes of epithelial cells secreting a thin cuticle which is thickened in places to form a spiral-running ridge, the *taenidium* (Fig. 1.1).

The taenidium prevents collapse of the tube but is reduced or absent in places where the walls of the tracheae

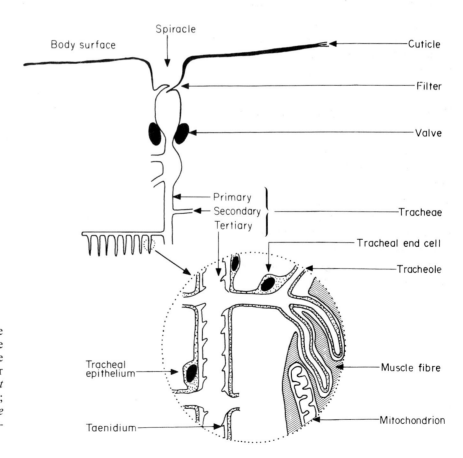

Fig. 1.1. Schematic illustration of the tracheal system in an insect. The large circle represents a magnified view of the circled portion the tertiary trachea (After Bursell, E. *An Introduction to Insect Physiology* (1970) Academic Press; Chapman, R. F. *The Insects: Structure and Function* (1969) The English Universities Press).

expand to form air sacs. The tracheae connect to the exterior via openings called *spiracles*. These are usually lateral in position often guarded by bristles or other structures to exclude dust (or water in aquatic insects) and in terrestrial insects can be closed by valves to limit water loss. Distally from the spiracles the tracheae branch to communicate with other parts of the tracheal system and eventually to form fine *tracheoles* in the tissues. The blind-ending tracheoles branching off from any one trachea all lie within a single palmate cell—the

tracheal end cell—and often become functionally, although not morphologically, intracellular in the tissues they supply. Oxygen is therefore brought into close proximity to the mitochondria (Fig. 1.1).

During rest the finest tracheal branches are filled with fluid but during muscular activity this is absorbed into the tissues. The mechanism by which this occurs is not understood but the effect is to reduce the liquid diffusion pathway for O_2 (oxygen) to the mitochondria, making O_2 more available to those tissues requiring it.

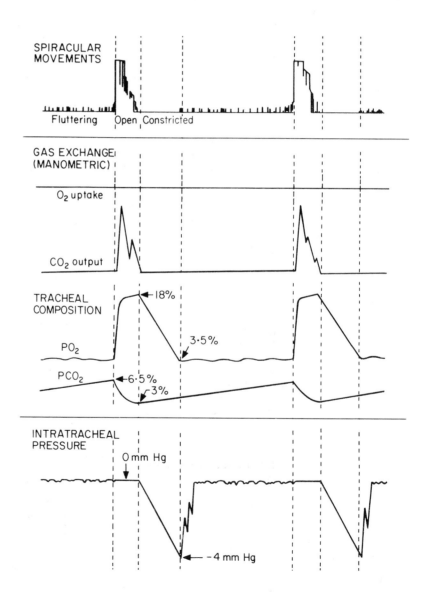

Fig. 1.2. Summary diagram showing the correlation between spiracular movements, gas exchange, intratracheal pressure and the composition of the tracheal gas (After Levy, R. I. & Schneiderman, H. A. (1966) *J. Insect Physiol.*, **12**, 465-492).

1.1.1 Ventilation during rest

The diffusion of O_2 from the spiracles to the tissues depends on the difference in partial pressure of O_2 between the atmosphere and the tracheole. In small insects (less than *c.*3 mm long) diffusion can provide sufficient O_2 to the flight muscles to support flight metabolism, but in larger insects diffusion alone is insufficient to meet the energy requirements during rest, let alone during flight. In large insects the diffusion pathways are therefore shortened by the primary tracheae being forcibly ventilated. During rest, pumping movements of the abdominal musculature provide this *ventilation*, and for many species the opening and closing of the spiracles is synchronized with the abdominal pumping strokes to produce a directional flow of air through the tracheal system. The control of the valves opening and closing the spiracles is complex but, in general, opening occurs in response to low levels of O_2 and high levels of carbon dioxide (CO_2).

Many resting insects release CO_2 in bursts followed by long intervals when little is released, although O_2-consumption remains constant throughout. The explanation for this cyclic CO_2-release lies in the behaviour of the spiracular valves. During release they are wide open and during the interburst period they close initially but subsequently open slightly and flutter. After the valves close at the end of a burst of CO_2-release, O_2-consumption reduces the intratracheal pressure because the CO_2 produced by respiration remains largely in solution as bicarbonate. Consequently, when the low O_2 content of the tracheal air and tissues, and the increased CO_2 in solution, eventually cause the spiracles to open minutely, fresh air will enter and replenish the O_2, causing the spiracles to close again. As the process repeats, the valves flutter until gaseous CO_2 increases to a critical point when the spiracles open fully and a burst of release is triggered (Fig. 1.2).

What is the rationale for periodic opening of the spiracles? Terrestrial insects are vulnerable to desiccation (§ 2.4.1) and many insects living in very dry environments have little dietary water. Pupae, for example, have no possibility of replacing lost water. Clearly, when the spiracles are closed, water loss from the tracheal system is nil; when they are open fully, it is maximal. The cyclic nature of CO_2-release is therefore an adaptation towards water conservation whereby water loss is restricted to the brief periods when the spiracles are fully open.

1.1.2. Ventilation during flight

In those species where little or no ventilation occurs, the primary tracheae often take the form of flattened air sacs, running alongside the muscles, and offer little

Fig. 1.3. The pattern of spiracular movement during rest **A** and flight **B** in *Schistocerca*. When the locust starts to fly, spiracles 1 and 4 to 10 (numbered from anterior to posterior) close and then open and close rhythmically. They are synchronized with abdominal ventilation movements and ensure an adequate supply of air to the central nervous system. Spiracles 2 and 3 remain wide open throughout flight, although they show incipient closing movements after some time (30 min into flight, **B**) and especially as flight deteriorates just before the termination of flight, **C**. These spiracles supply the flight muscles and therefore allow a tidal flow of air in and out of the thorax during thoracic pumping (After Miller, P. L. (1960) *J. exp. Biol.,* **37,** 264-278).

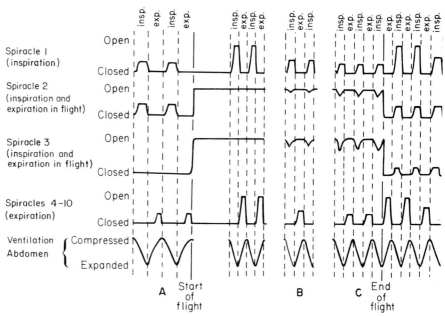

resistance to diffusion of oxygen into the secondary and tertiary tracheae (Fig. 1.1). In larger insects it is more common to find the primary trachea as a tube running axially through the centre of the muscle—thus shortening the diffusion pathways to the secondaries.

In bees, wasps and flies, the rate of abdominal ventilation may increase during flight but in many large insects it may decrease or even stop and be replaced by thoracic pumping. In locusts the small changes in the volume of the thorax caused by contractions of the wing muscles allow *c.* 5% of the air in the thorax to be exchanged with each wingstroke. The isolation of the thoracic and abdominal tracheal systems ensures that this exchange takes place with fresh air from outside and not with partially respired air from elsewhere in the tracheal system. When abdominal pumping continues during flight, the spiracles retain their synchronized opening and closing movements, but in species which rely on thoracic pumping, the appropriate spiracles remain open (Fig. 1.3).

1.2   RESPIRATION IN AQUATIC INSECTS

The tracheal respiratory system of insects is suitable primarily for respiration in air, and presumably evolved in air. Those species which have secondarily become aquatic have adopted several interesting adaptations to make the tracheal system suitable for gas exchange in water.

Some primitive insects, like mayflies and dragonflies, have aquatic larvae which retain the tracheal system but have non-functional spiracles. Oxygen diffuses from the water through the cuticle into the tracheal system, and often special areas of the cuticle, sometimes developed as extensions of the body surface (usually called gills), are richly tracheated to provide a large surface area for O_2-uptake. Many other aquatic insects retain functional spiracles. These insects, which usually take O_2 from the air above the water, must either visit the surface periodically or have some semi-permanent connection with the air. Larvae of the drone-fly, *Eristalis,* have a 'snorkel' tube which connects their terminal abdominal spiracles with the air at the surface. A hydrofuge (non-wetting) cuticle, or areas of hydrofuge hairs around the spiracles, helps this and similar insects to break the surface film tension during surfacing and prevents water entering the spiracles during diving. Many aquatic beetles and bugs take bubbles of air beneath the water as they dive. Water beetles such as *Dytiscus* have dorsally positioned abdominal spiracles which allow the space beneath the elytra to hold a large volume of air which is continuous with that in the tracheal system. Bugs, on the other hand, have ventrally placed spiracles and the sub-elytral space is of no use as a gas store. Consequently, many aquatic bugs swim only at the surface, and the diving species either have a snorkel, as in *Nepa,* the water scorpion or, like *Notonecta,* the water boatman, swim upside down.

The bubbles of air taken beneath the surface by aquatic insects act not so much as stores of O_2 but as *physical gills*. The hydrofuge hairs around the spiracles ensure that the bubbles of air have continuity with the air in the tracheal system and so, as the insect uses O_2 from the bubble, O_2 from the surrounding water diffuses into it. Nitrogen in the air diffuses out into the water but only at a third of the rate at which O_2 enters the bubble. Thus more O_2 is made available to the insect than was originally present in the bubble but eventually, as the bubble shrinks due to loss of nitrogen, the insect must return to the surface for a fresh supply. If the insect remains just below the surface, the gas pressure in the bubble will be maintained at approximately atmospheric pressure and nitrogen will diffuse out slowly. But if the insect takes the bubble to a greater depth, the pressure will increase by 0.1 atm for every metre of depth; speeding the diffusion of both O_2 and nitrogen out of the bubble. Thus the life of the bubble, and therefore the length of the dive, will depend not only on the initial size of the bubble and the insect's metabolic rate, but also on the depth to which the insect dives. If, however, the bubble were non-collapsible, the insect would not need to surface. Indeed, some aquatic insects need never visit the surface although they have physical gills which operate along similar principles to those described above. In the water bug *Aphelocheirus,* for example, the ventral surface of the body is covered in a pile of densely-packed fine hydrofuge hairs, the *plastron,* which hold a permanent non-collapsible thin film of air continuous with the air in the tracheal system. The plastron hairs are bent over at their tips and withstand up to four atmospheres before they collapse. In some beetles such as *Hydrophilus,* the water-scavenger, the plastron is supplemented by longer, less dense hairs which form a macroplastron. The air in the macroplastron is not permanent and must be renewed at the surface. Plastrons also occur on the surface of many insect eggs, both aquatic and terrestrial and in some aquatic pupae.

1.3 ENERGY METABOLISM

The immediate source of energy for muscular contraction is the hydrolysis of ATP. The ADP produced may be rephosphorylated in the short term by the use of arginine phosphate (acting like creatine phosphate in vertebrates) or, in the long term, by the oxidation of substances which we call *fuels*. It is perhaps because the aerobic oxidation of such fuels as carbohydrates, amino acids and fatty acids can proceed so efficiently in insects that there are no large stores of arginine phosphate in the flight muscles.

Two important questions arise: how do insects switch rapidly from resting to flight metabolism—during which the rate of respiration increases by as much as 100 times; and how is an adequate supply of suitable fuel made available to the flight muscles for flight metabolism to be maintained?

1.3.1 Pathways for the utilization of fuels in insect flight muscles

The molecular basis for contraction in muscles is similar in most animals and involves a sliding filament mechanism (§ 5.1). Contraction is initiated by depolarization of the *sarcoplasmic reticulum* (p. 74) (by the muscle fibre action potential which sweeps down the T system) and consequent release of Ca^{++} into the interior of the fibre which activates the myofibrillar ATP-ase (§ 5.2.2). Although ATP is the universal source of energy for contraction in all muscles, different species use different fuels for its regeneration. Blowflies and bees, for example, oxidize carbohydrate, while locusts and moths use mainly fats, and the tsetse fly and Colorado beetle use the imino acid proline.

1.3.2 Oxidation of carbohydrate in the blowfly

The glycerol-3-phosphate shuttle

The pathways of *glycolysis* and operation of the *TCA* (tricarboxylic acid) *cycle* in insect muscles are shown

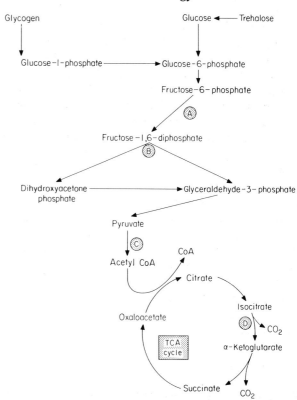

Fig. 1.4. The operation of the glycolytic pathway and TCA cycle in insects. **A** is phosphofructokinase (PFK); **B** is aldolase; **C** is pyruvate dehydrogenase (PDH); **D** is isocitrate dehydrogenase (ICDH).

in Fig. 1.4. The major insect specialization appears to be the possession of a 'G-3-P (glycerol-3-phosphate) *shuttle*' (Fig. 1.5). This shuttle is the most important mechanism for the re-oxidation of NADH produced during glycolysis. This is in contrast to the lactate dehydrogenase-catalyzed oxidation of NADH which operates in other muscles such as those in the legs. The importance of the G-3-P shuttle is due to the fact that the mitochondria are impermeable to NADH and NAD (and many other substances). G-3-P, however, is readily oxidized by the Ca^{++}-activated mitochondrial G-3-P dehydrogenase (Fig. 1.6) located on the outer surface of the inner mitochondrial membrane. During steady flight in the blowfly, mitochondrial oxidation of pyruvate and G-3-P occur at the same rate as these compounds are being formed. Thus, end products of glycolysis do not accumulate wastefully (cf. lactate accumulation in some exercising vertebrate muscles).

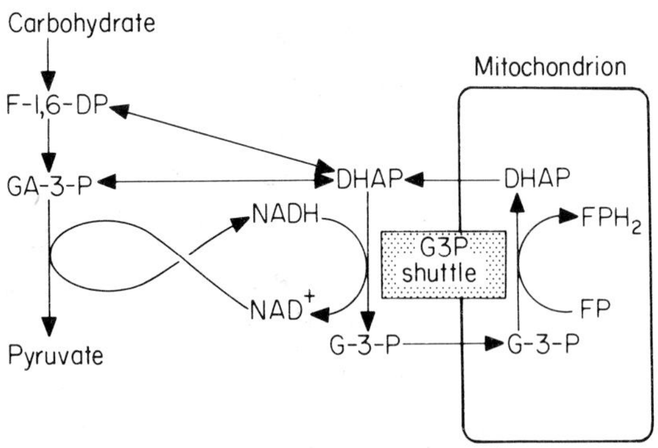

Carbohydrate

F-1,6-DP

GA-3-P

Pyruvate

NADH

NAD$^+$

DHAP

G3P shuttle

Mitochondrion

DHAP

FPH$_2$

FP

G-3-P

G-3-P

Fig. 1.5. The operation of the glycerol-3-phosphate shuttle in insect flight muscle. F-1,6-DP is fructose-1,6-diphosphate; GA-3-P is glyceraldehyde-3-phosphate; DHAP is dihydroxyacetone phosphate; G-3-P is glycerol-3-phosphate; FP is flavoprotein.

The control of glycolysis

In the blowfly, F-1,6-DP (fructose-1,6-diphosphate, see Fig. 1.4) and pyruvate show a dramatic increase in concentration on the initiation of flight. Both substances reach a peak in concentration within 1 min of the onset of flight but return to more-or-less pre-flight levels within 2-3 min. This suggests that although the production of these substances has been accelerated, the pathways for their further metabolism require activation

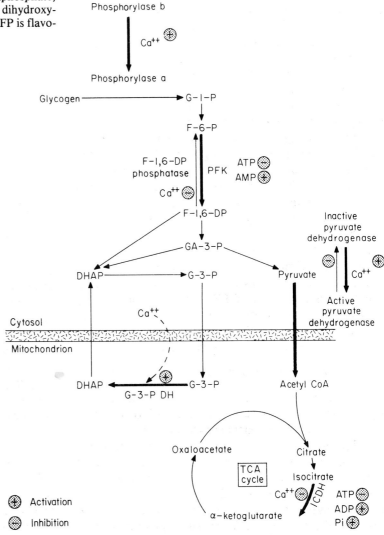

Fig. 1.6. Possible control points in energy metabolism in the blowfly. Heavy arrows indicate the predominant pathways.

during the transition from rest to flight and that this is subject to a short delay. Clues to the mechanisms whereby glycolysis is accelerated are gained from an examination of the changes in the concentrations of adenosine phosphates and inorganic ions such as Pi (inorganic phosphate) and Ca^{++}.

During flight, ATP decreases in concentration, whereas ADP, AMP, and Pi increase. The changes are rapid and a new steady state is achieved quickly. The change in the distribution of Ca^{++} within the muscle, mentioned earlier, may represent a 100-fold increase in the cytosolic concentration. The sarcoplasmic reticulum in the *asynchronous muscles* of the blowfly is relatively undeveloped by comparison with that of the *synchronous muscles* of the locust (§ 5.1) and the mitochondria are thought to be an important site for the release of Ca^{++} into the cytosol in asynchronous muscle. Can the changes in the concentrations of these metabolites and ions be responsible for increasing the rates of glycolysis and pyruvate oxidation? A key enzyme in the control of glycolysis is PFK (phosphofructokinase), and this must be activated during the transition from rest to flight (Fig. 1.4). PFK from insect flight muscles is inhibited by excess ATP but this can be overcome by AMP. A substrate cycle between F-6-P (fructose-6-phosphate) and F-1,6-DP increases the sensitivity to AMP since F-1,6-DP phosphatase (Fig. 1.6) is inhibited by AMP and Ca^{++}. The net flux from G-6-P to F-1,6-DP during rest is at a low level (despite a high residual activity of PFK) because of the activity of this phosphatase. During flight, the increases in AMP and Ca^{++} respectively cause simultaneous activation of PFK and inhibition of the phosphatase. The relative increase in the net flux in the direction of F-1,6-DP will be greater, therefore, than the relative increase in PFK activity.

The control of pyruvate oxidation

Pyruvate accumulates during the first few seconds of flight because it is produced faster than it is oxidized by the mitochondria. The enzyme pyruvate dehydrogenase (see Fig. 1.4) exists in an inactive and an active form (as it does in vertebrates) and the inactive form is converted to the active form by dephosphorylation under the action of a phosphatase which is activated by Ca^{++}. An interconversion cycle between the active and inactive forms of the enzyme works in an analogous way to

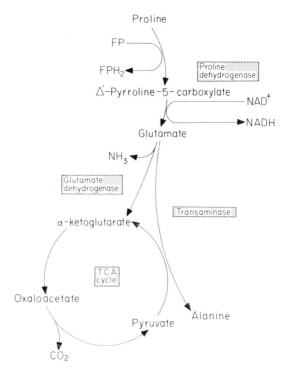

Fig. 1.7. Pathways for the partial oxidation of proline in flight muscles. The activity of glutamate dehydrogenase is higher in flight muscles of the tsetse fly and the Colorado beetle than in the blowfly.

the substrate cycle described above; the activity of pyruvate dehydrogenase is therefore very sensitive to pyruvate and Ca^{++}. Other factors could limit the rate of mitochondrial oxidation of pyruvate. It is thought that, initially, an enhanced rate of pyruvate oxidation may require a source of TCA cycle intermediates. On initiation of flight in the blowfly, alanine increases in concentration while proline decreases. Proline could act as a source of glutamate by the action of proline dehydrogenase (Fig. 1.7). ADP and pyruvate activate this enzyme but glutamate inhibits it. Thus the several-fold increase in pyruvate, together with the increase in ADP, stimulates proline oxidation to ensure that adequate levels of glutamate are maintained. Glutamate can be used for the transamination of pyruvate so that effectively proline enters the TCA cycle as α-ketoglutarate (Fig. 1.7) and provides a source of oxaloacetate allowing increased citrate synthesis.

A further rate limiting step in the oxidation of pyruvate

may be the need for activation of a TCA cycle enzyme. ICDH (isocitrate dehydrogenase) is a likely candidate since its activity is inhibited by ATP and Ca^{++}. ICDH is thought to be located in the fluid matrix of the mitochondria and would therefore be sensitive to intra-mitochondrial concentrations of Ca^{++}. Fig. 1.6 attempts to summarize how the factors discussed above could be acting in a concerted way to control flight metabolism in the blowfly. Although relating specifically to this species, the principles are probably relevant to most insect flight muscles. An exceptional case appears to be that of the tsetse fly, *Glossina*.

1.3.3   Proline oxidation in the tsetse fly

We have seen above how the blowfly uses small amounts of proline during the first few seconds of flight to supply TCA cycle intermediates. Many other insects may use proline in this way, but the tsetse fly appears unusual in that it uses proline as the major fuel for flight. The proposed pathway for its oxidation of proline is shown in Fig. 1.7. A high activity of proline dehydrogenase is characteristic of its flight muscles. The predominant pathway for glutamate is probably transamination with pyruvate to form alanine, but glutamate could also serve as a source of α-ketoglutarate under the action of the enzyme glutamate dehydrogenase (Fig. 1.7). This enzyme is inhibited by ATP and ammonia but subject to an activation by ADP and AMP which is dependent on the concentration of Pi. Thus the enzyme would be activated during the early seconds of flight but a build up of ammonia could soon exert an inhibiting effect. Nevertheless, the enzyme clearly has a potential to produce α-ketoglutarate during the early stages of flight (see also § 1.4.2).

1.3.4   Fatty acid oxidation in insects

The metabolic pathways involved in the oxidation of fatty acids appear to be common to insects and vertebrates and are outlined in Fig. 1.8. In most insects and vertebrates, the mitochondria are impermeable to the fatty-acyl-CoA thioesters of fatty acids, and carnitine-acetyl and parmitoyl transferases are associated with the walls of the mitochondria. These effect the transfer of fatty-acyl units into the mitochondria for β-oxidation and eventual entry of acetyl-CoA into the TCA cycle. It should be stressed that there is no known mechanism in any animal for the anaerobic oxidation of fats. Thus we encounter again the requirement of insects to undergo continuous muscular activity under aerobic conditions.

1.4   MAINTENANCE OF THE METABOLIC FUEL SUPPLY

In the blowfly and locust, breakdown of flight muscle glycogen is initiated at the onset of flight by the conversion of the inactive form of glycogen phosphorylase into the active form (Fig. 1.6). Although endogenous fuel in the flight muscles will support flight for only relatively short periods, its oxidation enables flights to be undertaken readily. More importantly, it also allows time for the activation of fuel-releasing machinery elsewhere (for example in the fat body) to ensure that adequate supplies of fuel enter the blood for transport to the flight muscles during long flights. In the tsetse fly, glycogen

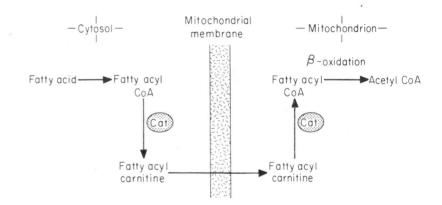

Fig. 1.8. The pathways of lipid utilization by muscle. Cat is carnitine acyl transferase. There are two types of acyl transferases; carnitine-acetyl and carnitine-palmitoyl transferases for short and long chain fatty acids respectively.

is present in minimal quantities and proline provides the ready source of fuel, being present in the flight muscle in relatively high concentration.

In insects, the tissues are bathed in blood, the circulation of which is effected largely without blood vessels. It is moved about the haemocoel by a combination of tidal flow, caused by the movements of the animal, and pumping by the single dorsal aorta that runs from the tip of the abdomen to the head, though there are often also accessory pumps at the bases of the legs and antennae. Since there is no capillary system, the impregnation of the flight muscles with a large volume of extracellular fluid in the space surrounding the tracheoles and *T-system* (§ 5.1.1) keeps diffusion distances for the passage of fuels from the blood to the muscles as small as possible. In addition, a steep concentration gradient is maintained between the blood and the muscle. Consequently, the concentrations of fuels in the blood of insects are characteristically much higher than in vertebrates. This may also be necessary to saturate the enzymes involved in the first steps of metabolism when the inadequacies of the circulation allow small local fluctuations in fuel concentration to occur.

1.4.1   The supply of carbohydrate to the flight muscles in blowflies

The endogenous glycogen in the flight muscles supports flight metabolism for only 10-15 min. Thereafter trehalose from the blood is the main fuel, although sugars from the crop may also contribute. In flies which have been maintained on water for 24 h, and in which the crop is therefore empty, the concentration of blood trehalose remains constant at 22 μg.μl^{-1} throughout a 50-min-flight.

The main stores of glycogen are in the fat body and intestinal wall. Little is known about the control of glycogen breakdown in the latter, but fat body glycogenolysis is under endocrine control. A *hyperglycaemic hormone*, secreted by the neurosecretory cells of the *corpus cardiacum* (§ 3.3.1) shortly after the onset of flight (Fig. 1.9), activates the kinase which converts the inactive phosphorylase (**B** in Fig. 1.4) to the active form. If release of the hormone is prevented by cutting the nerves between the brain and the corpus cardiacum, the quantity of blood trehalose falls rapidly during flight (initially at about 10μg.min^{-1}, but decreasing as

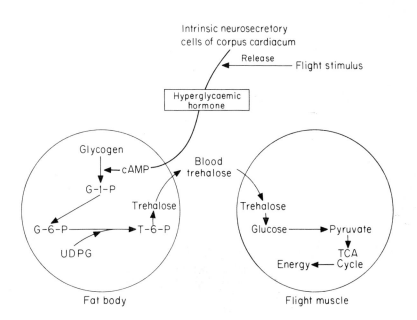

Fig. 1.9. The endocrine control of flight metabolism in the blowfly (see Vejbjerg, K. & Normann, T.C. (1974) *J. Insect Physiol.*, **20**, 1189-1192).

wingbeat frequency declines) until flight eventually stops. In response to the hyperglycaemic hormone, the maximum rate of mobilization of trehalose in resting flies is also of the order of $10\,\mu g.min^{-1}$. If similar rates of trehalose mobilization occur during flight, these observations explain how the blowfly achieves a steady-state concentration of blood trehalose during flight.

1.4.2   The supply of proline to the flight muscles in tsetse flies

Proline is oxidized during flight at a relatively high rate initially (c. $70\text{-}80\,\mu g.min^{-1}$) but this decreases rapidly within 2-3 min as the pool of available proline decreases. Flight muscle proline would support the high initial rate of oxidation for only c. 90 s, and that in the blood for perhaps another 30 s. Proline is synthesized in the abdomen during flight but the maximum rate of synthesis (c. $7\,\mu g.min^{-1}$) appears inadequate to prolong flight for any significant time. Consequently, proline oxidation can support flight for only 2-3 min. In the laboratory, some species when supported on a flight mill, can fly for longer periods. It may be that fuels other than proline are used to supply energy to the flight muscles, but it has been shown recently that such individuals may fly longer because they start flight with higher than normal reserves of proline.

It has been suggested that the dependence of the tsetse fly on proline oxidation is related to its exclusive blood-feeding habit, a diet rich in protein but low in carbohydrate. However, the recent demonstration that the Colorado beetle, a herbivore, also uses proline as a major fuel during flight, makes such an argument appear redundant.

1.4.3   The supply of carbohydrate and fat to the flight muscles in locusts

In the locust, flight muscle glycogen could support flight for only 2-3 min. This may be adequate to support short flights from one plant to another but for longer flights other sources of fuel are used. Stores of tissue glycogen are meagre; e.g. in *Locusta*, c. $400\,\mu g$ in the fat body and $150\,\mu g$ in the wall of the hind-gut. The blood, however, contains about 6 mg of trehalose. This is therefore the largest pool of available carbohydrate. By contrast, the quantity of lipid in the blood is modest, c. 2 mg, whereas in the fat body it may exceed 10 mg.

How does the locust control the mobilization and use of these energy stores?

Trehalose utilization

The changes in blood carbohydrate, fat body glycogen and blood diglyceride during flight are shown in Fig. 1.10. Trehalose is used by the flight muscles at a rate of

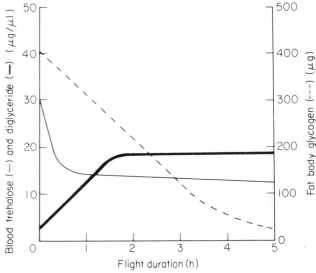

Fig. 1.10. The effect of flight on the blood and tissue metabolites in *Locusta migratoria* (After Jutsum, A. R. & Goldsworthy, G. J. (1976) *J. Insect Physiol.,* **22**, 243-249).

c. $120\,\mu g.min^{-1}$ during the first 10 min, falling to $c.10\,\mu g.min^{-1}$ after 30 min. To understand why this occurs when only half of the blood trehalose has been utilized one must look at the control of lipid mobilization and oxidation.

Diglyceride mobilization and oxidation

In the fat body, lipid consists mainly of triglyceride but, once mobilized, it is carried in the blood as diglyceride. These hydrophobic diglycerides are carried attached to special blood lipoproteins which are already present in the blood before mobilization and can carry extra diglyceride from the fat body. Lipid mobilization during flight is under endocrine control (Fig. 1.11). Within 2 min of the onset of flight a hormone, AKH (*adipokinetic hormone;* Fig. 1.12), is released from the corpora cardiaca (§ 3.3.1) and stimulates the breakdown of fat body triglyceride.

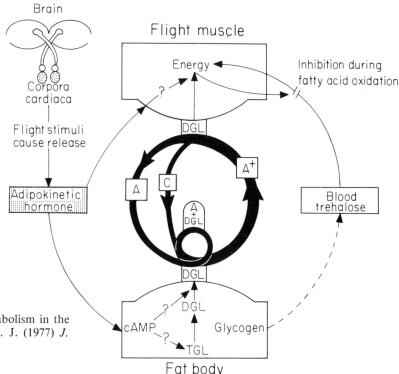

Fig. 1.11. The endocrine control of flight metabolism in the locust (see Mwangi, R. W. & Goldsworthy, G. J. (1977) *J. comp. Physiol.*, **114**, 177-190).

At rest, the lipoproteins in the blood (see Fig. 1.11, lipoprotein A) carry *c.* 3 $g.\mu l^{-1}$ of diglyceride, but in response to the action of AKH these form a new complex (lipoprotein A^+ in Fig. 1.11) which can carry up to 40 $g.\mu l^{-1}$. This new lipoprotein complex is the effective substrate for the flight muscles. A and A^+ shuttle back and forth between the fat body and the flight muscles carrying diglyceride. The maximum rate of diglyceride mobilization from the fat body is *c.* 115 $\mu g.^{-1}$ and the rate of its oxidation in the flight muscles is *c.* 85 $\mu g.^{-1}$. Clearly, the fat body can supply diglyceride to the flight muscles in sufficient quantity to maintain flight for long periods.

PCA-Leu-Asn-Phe-Thr-Pro-Asn-Trp-Gly-Thr-NH$_2$

Fig. 1.12. The structure of locust adipokinetic hormone. The decapeptide has the cyclic form of glutamic acid at the N-terminal and an amide at the C-terminal. This is the first insect neurohormone to be characterized (after Stone, J. *et al.* (1976) *Nature*, **263**, 207-211).

AKH stimulates the oxidation by the flight muscles of fatty acids derived from A^+ lipoprotein (Fig. 1.11). It is this increased fatty acid oxidation which reduces the rate of trehalose oxidation. This situation is similar to that in vertebrate cardiac muscle, where glucose utilization during starvation is reduced by the oxidation of fatty acids. In vertebrates, PFK (Fig. 1.4) is inhibited by the increased concentrations of extra-mitochondrial citrate that occur during fatty acid oxidation. In insects, however, PFK is not sensitive to citrate (although it is in other arthropods). The point at which glycolytic inhibition occurs in locust flight muscle during lipid oxidation is uncertain, but the enzyme aldolase (Fig. 1.4) appears to be a good candidate since it is citrate sensitive. In the locust, therefore, glycolytic flux may be reduced during fatty acid oxidation in an analogous manner to that in vertebrates. This spares blood sugar from use by the flight muscles, leaving it for tissues such as the brain and nervous system, which have a continuous requirement for glucose.

Further reading

Bailey E. (1975) Biochemistry of Insect Flight. Part 2. Fuel Supply. *Ibid,* pp. 91-176.

Crabtree B. & Newsholme E. A. (1975) Comparative aspects of fuel utilization and metabolism by muscle. In *Insect Muscle* (Ed. P. N. R. Usherwood), pp. 405-500, Academic Press, London.

Miller P. L. (1974) Respiration—aerial gas transport. In *The Physiology of Insects* (Ed. M. Rockstein) **VI**, pp. 355-402, Academic Press, New York.

Sacktor B. (1975) Biochemistry of Insect Flight. Part 1. Utilization of fuels by muscle. In *Insect Biochemistry and Function* (Ed. D. J. Candy & B. A. Kilby) pp. 3-88, Chapman and Hall, London.

Chapter 2
Transporting Tissues

2.1 EPITHELIAL FUNCTION

Insects may be thought of as consisting of sheets and tubes of epithelia which separate compartments and fluids of different and varying composition. The maintenance of these fluids depends upon selective movement of molecules between them and also between them and the external environment. Molecules cross membranes primarily by two distinct processes. One is *passive transport* which does not require a direct supply of energy; the other is *active transport* which does. In passive transport, molecules move down a concentration gradient across a membrane into a region of lower concentration. Active transport mechanisms move molecules in the opposite direction, i.e. from regions of low to regions of high concentration. The operation of both mechanisms may involve selectivity in that certain molecules cross membranes more easily than others. Such specificity is due not only to the physico-chemical characteristics of the membrane but also to the selectivity of carrier molecules. Cell membranes consist of an organized mixture of polar lipids, carbohydrates and proteins. The lipid bi-layer of the plasma membrane is impermeable to all compounds except those which are lipid soluble and these compounds diffuse across readily. However, in both passive and active transport, many lipid-insoluble molecules, such as electrolytes, amino acids and carbohydrates, also cross the membrane, either via its non-lipid components or via carrier molecules.

The general mechanisms for the transport of solute and solvent are as follows. Ions may be moved across membranes by *ion exchange pumps*. In neutral pumps there is a one-for-one exchange of cations and no potential difference is generated across the membrane. *Electrogenic pumps* (i.e. those which generate electro-potentials) also exist and these pump specific ions against gradients e.g. K^+ pumps in Malpighian tubules and salivary glands (§ 2.2.4 and § 2.3.1). The movement of water across epithelia may seem difficult to understand but the basic mechanisms are fairly simple. Much of the fluid flow across an epithelium is generated by the transport of solutes. This phenomenon is of fundamental importance and, in tissues such as the insect rectum, permits water to be moved against steep osmotic gradients. Fluid transport can also occur by pinocytosis, that is the formation of vesicles of fluid by membrane invagination. However, although important in some tissues, this process lacks sufficient specificity and large amounts of fluid can be transported only if continuous, rapid synthesis of cell membranes occurs.

It is clear from Figs. 2.3, 2.7, 2.9 and 2.14 that cells concerned with transporting fluids and solutes have similarities in their ultrastructural organization, especially with respect to the extensive infoldings of either

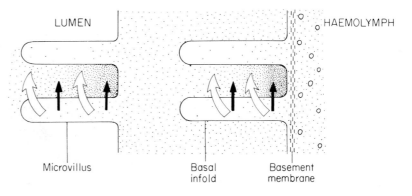

Fig. 2.1. Standing gradient model. Black arrows, active transport of solutes; white arrows, osmotic flow of water. Concentration of solute occurs within the basal infoldings and within the narrow channels between the microvilli. These standing gradients are indicated by the density of stippling; this is greatest at the blind ends of the channels. Water is transported from the haemolymph to the lumen.

the basal or the apical membranes, or both of them. A number of suggestions have been put forward to explain how these infoldings act. In *standing gradient models* (Fig. 2.1), solutes are pumped into blind-ending channels and create regions of localized high concentration. Water then moves into the channel by osmosis and emerges from the open end of the channel as either iso-osmotic or hyper-osmotic fluid. This model adequately explains the transport of water in, e.g., the vertebrate gall bladder because of its long channels. In tissues with short channels, discrete areas for pumping ions have been proposed. In insect Malpighian tubules, the channels present on the basal surface of the cell and those in the brush border (Fig. 2.7) are not extensive enough to generate the gradients necessary for the observed flow of solvent. Moreover, histochemistry at the electron microscope level has revealed localized pumps.

It should be emphasized that these models are not yet proven and the solutes involved have been considered to be more or less exclusively monovalent ions. However, recent research involving electron probe analysis has failed to demonstrate high concentrations of ions at the ends of the channels. Indeed, the gradient across the tissue is the reverse of the expected values and the cytoplasm in the basal channels has a lower ionic concentration than the general cell cytoplasm. Gradients may exist but may be generated by organic solutes and not by monovalent ions. It is also possible that electrogenic pumps in the folded membranes may cause *electro-endosmotic* flow of water; this is the flow of water across a charged membrane when a potential difference is generated, e.g. by the secretion of K^+, and under these circumstances hypo-osmotic fluid may be secreted. For example, a potential difference of -50 mV is equivalent in driving force to an osmotic gradient of 100 mosmol. Thus, although the validity of the standing gradient theory is doubted the general principle that water movement is linked to solute transport is still tenable.

2.2   THE GUT

The insect intestine (Fig. 2.2) is not a simple tube from mouth to anus; it contains diverticula and often doubles back on itself. The mid-gut arises embryonically from endoderm, whereas the fore- and hind-guts are ectodermal, and are lined with cuticle that is continuous with that covering the body surface. The cuticular lining of the mid-gut, the peritrophic membrane, differs from the rest of the cuticle (p. 27). The gut is concerned not only with the digestion and absorption of food but also has a specialized role in controlling water balance and excretion to an extent not found in other animals.

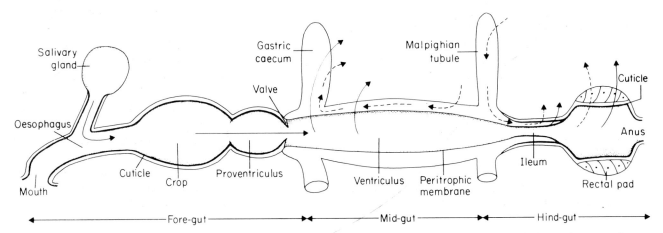

Fig. 2.2. The main regions of the gut in insects; many variations occur and in different insects particular regions may be extensively modified and adapted. The arrows show movement of endogenous (dotted) and exogenous (solid) fluid within the alimentary canal. Absorptive cycles occur in the caeca, and excretory cycles in the Malpighian tubules and hind-gut. It is possible for digestion to occur along the length of the mid-gut but the products of digestion are swept forward into the caeca (After Berridge, M. J. (1970). *Insect Ultrastructure* ed. A. C. Neville. *Symp. R. ent. Soc., Lond.* 135-151).

2.2.1 Nutrition and digestion

Insects eat a wider variety of foodstuffs than any other group of animals; their diets include decaying organic materials, leaves, animal and plant fluids, nectar, wood, hair, feathers, and even wax. The adaptations of different species to their different diets has markedly influenced not only the morphology and physiology of the digestive tract but also the physiology and behaviour of the insect as a whole. In insects, as in other animals, foodstuffs may be digested first physically and then chemically into sub-units to facilitate absorption into the blood stream. The extent of the physical phase of digestion varies considerably, being extensive in insects with cutting and biting mouthparts, and non-existent in fluid feeders. The enzymes responsible for the chemical phase of digestion occur in the saliva and mid-gut secretions as well as within the mid-gut tissues; in many species much of the chemical digestion is performed by gut micro-organisms.

Extra-intestinal chemical digestion may also occur, e.g. in the larvae of some Neuroptera and Coleoptera. *Dytiscus* larvae inject mid-gut enzymes through channels in the mandibles into the body of their prey. The prey's tissues are then histolysed prior to ingestion. Many fluid-feeding insects secrete substances which similarly facilitate ingestion, though such secretions are not digestive in the strict sense. In aphids, the salivary glands are thought to secrete a galacturonidase which digests the middle lamella between the plant cells and thus facilitates penetration of the mouthparts into the phloem bundles. Blood-sucking insects secrete saliva into the wound to increase the host's blood flow at the wound and sometimes also to act as an anticoagulant.

Digestion in insects, as in other metazoa, is both extra- and intra-cellular; the final stages of chemical digestion of the food occur within the cells of the mid-gut. The initial stages, however, occur in the gut lumen, predominantly in the mid-gut, or in some species in the fore-gut. Enzymes in the fore-gut may be products of the salivary glands or be regurgitated from the mid-gut. The enzymes present in both saliva and the mid-gut are adapted to the diet of the insect. In general carnivores possess proteases and lipases, whereas herbivores possess predominantly carbohydrases. In non-feeding stages, such as short-lived adult Lepidoptera, no enzymes are detectable in the mid-gut.

The carbohydrases, proteases and lipases present in insects are in general similar in properties to those in vertebrates. The exceptions are that insect proteases are not released as inactive precursors so, for example, there is no equivalent of trypsinogen. In addition insect gut pH levels range from only 6.5 to 7.5, so that the proteases are trypsin-like rather than pepsin-like. Special adaptations occur in species that are able to digest proteins such as silk, collagen and keratin which are resistant to hydrolysis. In clothes moth larvae (*Tineola*) hydrolysis of keratin is achieved by cysteine reductase. In the low redox potential of the larval mid-gut, this reduces the di-sulphide bridges in the cysteine residues which bind adjacent polypeptide chains in the keratin molecule. The polypeptides, now with free -SH groups, are attacked by proteases which, unlike the tryptic proteases of other animals, are not inhibited by -SH groups. The low redox potential is maintained by the unusually poor tracheal supply. This is a striking example of physiological adaptation to specialized diet.

Digestion of cellulose

Cellulose is a long chain polysaccharide formed from glucose units joined by β-1,4 links which render it resistant to hydrolysis. Herbivores which are able to digest cellulose in addition to starch have a significant dietary bonus in the extra glucose which is made available. However, in the insects, as in other groups, only a few species are able to digest cellulose. The digestion may be effected by enzymes produced by the insect or by gut micro-organisms. Two enzymes are involved in the complete digestion of cellulose: a cellulase which breaks down the cellulose into the disaccharide cellobiose, and a hemi-cellulase (cellobiase) which releases glucose from the disaccharide. Scolytids (bark beetles) lack a cellulase but possess a cellobiase, the larvae pass large amounts of wood through the gut to obtain sufficient food from the cell contents. On the other hand, species such as death-watch and wood-worm beetles and the silverfish, *Ctenolepisma,* digest cellulose completely. In these examples microorganisms are not involved but, in other groups, the use of symbionts to digest cellulose is widespread. Termites, which produce no cellulases are perhaps the most closely-studied example. In primitive termites, cellulose is digested by cellulases from large populations of flagellates housed in special diverticula of the hind-gut. The protozoans are lost when the hind-gut is shed at each moult. The infection is maintained by proctodaeal feeding. In *Zootermopsis* the symbionts digest the cellulose to acetates and there is a shift in metabolism so that the termite is able to utilize C_2 carbon skeletons rather than C_6 sugars.

2.2.2 Absorption

The absorption of digested food is thought to occur mainly in the mid-gut, though this has been studied in only a few species. In *Periplaneta* and *Schistocerca* the absorption of sugars, tri-glycerides and amino acids occurs predominantly in the mid-gut caeca. An important factor in the regulation of absorption is the rate at which the crop empties. Crop emptying is an exponential function; with a constant proportion of the crop contents being released into the mid-gut per unit of time. Furthermore, the rate of crop emptying is inversely proportional to the osmotic pressure of the crop contents. Thus, irrespective of the concentration in the crop, food is passed into the mid-gut in a constant amount. This regulation depends upon the osmolarity and not the chemical nature of the solution, because iso-osmotic solutions of glucose, sorbose, glycerol and NaCl, produced similar rates of crop emptying. The osmoreceptors have not been described but the pathway involved in the control of crop emptying is presumed to be osmoreceptors → frontal ganglion → ingluvial ganglion → proventricular valve.

Carbohydrate absorption

The principal haemolymph sugar in most insects is trehalose which is a disaccharide of glucose. A concentration gradient exists between the gut lumen and the haemolymph for any monosaccharides present in the gut. Passive diffusion is effective in absorbing glucose from the lumen into the haemolymph until equilibrium is reached. *In vivo* this equilibrium position is shifted by the conversion of glucose in the haemolymph into trehalose by the fat body. This removal of glucose maintains the concentration gradient and the situation is quite different from that in mammals where glucose uptake is linked with the active transport of Na^+. In insects the process of *facilitated diffusion* is not enhanced by ions and energy is not expended at the site of uptake but by the fat body in the conversion to trehalose.

Lipid absorption

The actual composition of the lipids absorbed, especially glycerides, is not known with certainty. Free fatty acids, glycerol and emulsified lipids can all be absorbed. The slightly alkaline pH of the gut and the occurrence of free fatty acids, either in the diet or liberated by the action of lipases, will emulsify the glycerides present in the diet. Fatty acids can be demonstrated in the crop epithelium but experiments with ^{14}C-palmitin in known ratios with the inert dye amaranth demonstrate that absorption occurs mainly in the mid-gut caecae.

Amino acid absorption

Proteins are probably absorbed from the gut lumen as small peptides and amino acids are liberated intracellularly in the gut epithelium. However, only the uptake of free amino acids has been examined. Insects are unusual in that they possess high concentrations of free amino acids in their haemolymph (§ 5.2.1). Thus absorption must occur against adverse concentration gradients. The problem has been investigated in *Schistocerca* by filling the intestine along its whole length with solutions of radio-labelled amino acids and iodinated albumen, which were iso-osmotic to the haemolymph. By sampling the haemolymph and the contents of the caeca it was established that labelled amino acids rapidly entered the haemolymph. However, the concentration of total amino acid within the caeca increased rapidly to a level above that in the haemolymph. It is suggested that the absorption of amino acids is brought about by the movement of water out of the gut lumen at a more rapid rate than the movement of amino acids. However, differences in the rate of uptake of some amino acids have been reported and selective and active uptake processes may exist also.

2.2.3 Flux of water and ions across the gut wall

The intestine is a major site for the uptake of ions and water and their exchange with the haemolymph. Two different aspects are involved; one is concerned with functions of the Malpighian tubules and rectum and the second with feeding, digestion and absorption.

The rapid uptake of water from the gut lumen (§ 2.2.2) will facilitate the absorption of all foodstuffs by concentrating all the gut contents and enhancing diffusion

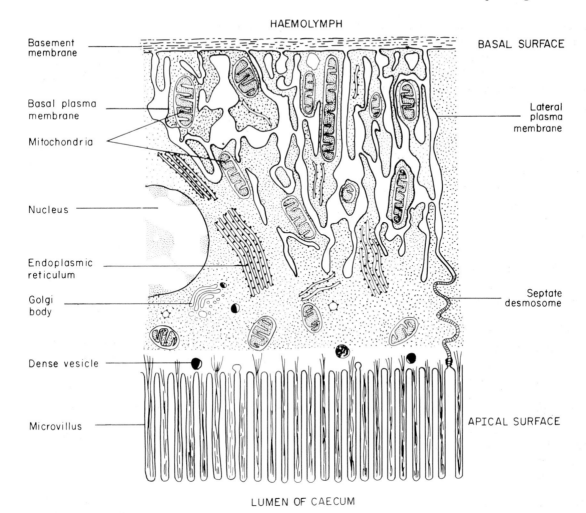

HAEMOLYMPH

BASAL SURFACE

Basement
membrane

Basal plasma
membrane

Mitochondria

Lateral
plasma
membrane

Nucleus

Endoplasmic
reticulum

Golgi
body

Septate
desmosome

Dense vesicle

Microvillus

APICAL SURFACE

LUMEN OF CAECUM

Fig. 2.3. Typical absorptive cell in a mid-gut caecum. Many microvilli are present on the apical membrane and the basement membrane is extensively infolded (After Berridge, M. J. (1970); see Fig. 2.2.).

gradients between the lumen and the haemolymph. The organization of a typical mid-gut cell is shown in Fig. 2.3. The movement of water out of the lumen is linked to the transport of Na^+ pumped from the cell into the haemolymph and replaced by Na^+ entering the cell from the lumen. This uni-directional movement of ions occurs because the apical membrane of the cell (i.e. that on the lumen side) is much more permeable than the basal membrane. When the cardiac glycoside ouabain (a specific inhibitor of Na^+/K^+-linked ATPase pumps) is placed on the haemolymph side of a gut *in vitro* preparation the normal potential difference due to active Na^+ transport across the gut wall (haemolymph positive) is lost. Ouabain is ineffective if placed in the lumen, which suggests that the pump is situated on the basal membrane (Fig. 2.3). Numerous mitochondria are associated with the infoldings of this and presumably supply energy for the pump. This movement of Na^+ generates an osmotic flow of water that drags other solutes through the cell into the haemolymph and concentrates less mobile materials in the gut, so facilitating their passive diffusion.

This mechanism occurs in the caeca but it seems that other mechanisms operate elsewhere in the mid-gut. Ions are removed from the lumen of other regions but the use of radio-labelled inulin (which cannot penetrate the gut wall) has shown that there is no net movement of water. Metabolic inhibitors stop this ion transport, but allow water flux from the lumen by osmosis. Thus, there is a mechanism present which normally prevents the efflux of water. The impermeability of the posterior regions of the mid-gut may facilitate the movements of fluid from the gut into the caeca and thus aid absorption (Fig. 2.2).

Goblet cells

Goblet cells are found in the mid-gut of certain larval Lepidoptera and Trichoptera. These differ in function from the goblet cells of vertebrate guts, their role being to secrete K^+ from the haemolymph into the gut lumen. In the silkworm, *Hyalophora,* the isolated mid-gut transports K^+ at a rate of 20 μequiv. $cm^{-2} h^{-1}$, which can maintain a potential difference of up to 100 mV (lumen positive) for many hours. The transporting mechanism is insensitive to ouabain and probably consists of an electrogenic pump which secretes K^+ into the cavity of the goblet cell which opens to the gut lumen. This secretion of K^+ by the mid-gut is a specialization which does not occur in all insects.

2.2.4   Salivary glands

The saliva of insects, in addition to being concerned with feeding and digestion (§ 2.2.1), is used to lubricate the food during ingestion and to clean the mouthparts, and is often an important component in the total water balance of the insect. In the adult blowfly, the salivary glands are a pair of long tubes extending the length of the body. Most of the tube is of one cell type characterized by large secretory canaliculi formed from invaginations of the apical plasma membrane, the surface of which is covered with microvilli. Infoldings in the basement membrane are associated with numerous mitochondria. These secretory cells, when stimulated *in vitro,* secrete a potassium-rich fluid which is iso-osmotic with the haemolymph. A short segment between the secretory region and the salivary duct re-absorbs this potassium from the saliva, and the saliva secreted finally is hypo-osmotic to the haemolymph.

The secretory region of the salivary glands in *Calliphora* can be stimulated to secrete *in vitro* by 5-hydroxytrypta-mine (5-HT) providing a useful model for analysis of the mechanisms by which cells respond to stimulants and hormones. The specificity and degree of the cell's response to 5-HT depends on a precise bonding between the indole ring, its hydroxyl group and the receptor on the cell membrane. The first effect of 5-HT upon the gland is to increase the intracellular levels of calcium probably by increasing the permeability of the basal plasma membrane. There is a simultaneous activation of the enzyme adenylate cyclase and an increase in the intracellular level of cyclic 3′,5′-AMP. Cyclic AMP stimulates K^+ transport, modulates Ca^{++} influx, and increases the flow of Cl^- across the apical membrane (Fig. 2.4). Water follows the movement of the ions. It should be stressed, however, that there is little evidence that 5-HT is a regulatory agent of the salivary gland *in vivo.*

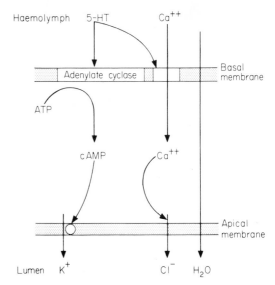

Fig. 2.4. A possible scheme for the action of 5-HT in increasing fluid secretion by the salivary glands in *Calliphora.* Both the production of cAMP and entry of Ca^{++} are affected by 5-HT. The increase in cAMP stimulates the K^+ pump; Ca^{++} controls the transport of Cl^-. Water movements follow the transport of K^+ and Cl^-.

2.3 EXCRETORY SYSTEMS

Insects, in common with many other invertebrates, are much more tolerant of changes in the levels of their body fluid components than are vertebrates. Nevertheless, efficient mechanisms operate to maintain the levels of ions, water and other metabolites within tolerated limits. In terrestrial insects, the major system for regulating water balance and concentrations and complements of ions, as well as for the removal of metabolic waste products, is the Malpighian tubule—hind-gut system; the functions of excretion and homeostasis of ions and water are intimately connected. In aquatic insects, however, special regions of the cuticle, e.g. the anal papillae in mosquito larvae, may also be important. Thus, the Malpighian tubules and rectum, either separately or together, must conserve ions and water at some times, and at other times ensure their removal from the body; at all times excretory products must be eliminated from the haemolymph. There is no concise chemical definition of excretion; it is the separation and elimination from the body of metabolic wastes. However, some compounds may be useful metabolically at one time but not at others, and some may be used quite differently by different species. Some terrestrial insects have to avoid the loss of salts and water but others, especially fluid feeders, experience periods of excess water intake when water has to be eliminated. Likewise, freshwater insects need to promote water loss while minimizing loss of ions, whereas brackish water insects need to conserve water but eliminate salts, and estuarine species have to cope with fluctuating salinities.

2.3.1 Malpighian tubule functioning

The Malpighian tubules form a primary urine and are in many ways analogous to the glomerulus of the mammalian kidney. They produce, by passive secretion and specific active transport systems, a continuous flow of fluid. This primary urine is iso-osmotic with the haemolymph and contains all the small molecular weight materials present in haemolymph. However, the composition of the urine voided finally from the anus is affected by reabsorptive mechanisms found in the tubules and in the rectum. Although lacking a counter-current system (but see § 2.3.4), the insects are capable of

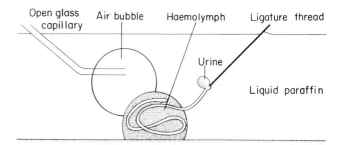

Fig. 2.5. Arrangement used to study secretion in an isolated Malpighian tubule. The tubule is contained in a drop of haemolymph or saline. The proximal end is severed at the junction with the hind-gut, and this end is ligatured off and pulled out of the droplet. Urine is collected from a nick in the tubule. Discrete droplets are formed because the preparation is covered in liquid paraffin (After Ramsay, J. A. (1954) *J. exp. Biol.,* **31,** 104-113).

producing a hyper-osmotic urine by secretion and reabsorption.

The formation of urine in insects has been investigated extensively in isolated Malpighian tubules, using the technique illustrated in Fig. 2.5. This allows measurements to be made of the effects of the composition of the bathing medium upon the composition and rate of formation of the primary urine. Analysis of the ionic composition and osmotic pressure (OP) has to be made on nanolitre samples of secreted fluid. The results of such experiments show the OP of the urine to be nearly always iso-osmotic with the bathing fluid, but the ionic content to be different (Table 2.1). Usually the K^+

	Concentrations of bathing fluids and urines (mM.l^{-1}).		
	Bathing Fluid	*Carausius Schistocerca Tipula Calliphora*	*Rhodnius*
Na^+	142	20	90
K^+	20	145	95
Cl^-	126	155	180
$H_2PO_4^-$	7	20	< 1
Glucose	20	8	5

Table 2.1 Composition of the primary urine produced by Malpighian tubules of several insects; values given are approximate.

concentrations are much higher and Na$^+$ concentrations much lower than in the bathing fluid, but *Rhodnius* differs with respect to Na$^+$ (see below). Potassium ions are actively pumped into the tubule lumen, Cl$^-$ ions following passively (or they may be actively secreted in some insects). It is the active secretion of ions, especially K$^+$, by electrogenic pumps that is of the utmost importance in urine formation. If K$^+$ ions are absent from the *in vitro* bathing fluid, urine secretion falls to a low rate.

Rhodnius produces little or no urine between its intermittent blood feeds, and tubules isolated from nonfeeding insects are inactive. Within 2-3 h of feeding, the insect voids its own weight in urine, and this is regulated by a diuretic hormone (§ 2.4.1). The excretory physiology of *Rhodnius* has been investigated extensively but only through the study of stimulated isolated tubules. In other species, resting tubules secrete urine at a significant rate, however, and information has been gained both from these and from stimulated tubules. In *Rhodnius* and in some other insects, a specific Na$^+$ pump is present in addition to K$^+$ and Cl$^-$ pumps. This means that *Rhodnius* tubules can produce

urine in the absence of K$^+$, if Na$^+$ ions are present. In the tsetse fly, *Glossina,* the driving ions are Na$^+$, K$^+$ being required only to maintain a high intracellular potassium concentration. It is likely that different species use the pumps to differing extents.

Malpighian tubules are freely permeable to organic solutes of low molecular weight, in some insects to molecules as large as inulin. Organic solutes may be passively or actively secreted into the tubule lumen, providing a mechanism for the removal of unwanted materials from the haemolymph. Some insects have the ability to secrete toxins actively, which may enable the insect to feed on poisonous plants. In *Rhodnius,* each of the four tubules has a lower (reabsorptive segment) proximal to the gut which reabsorbs K$^+$; the K$^+$ in the urine is 4 mM (the same as in the haemolymph) whereas that in the primary urine is 70-90 mM. In other insects, two distinct cell types occur, intermingled throughout the length of the tubule. In *Calliphora* the more numerous primary cells (Fig. 2.6) are thought to be secretory and the stellate cells to be reabsorptive. In other species the different roles of the two cell types are

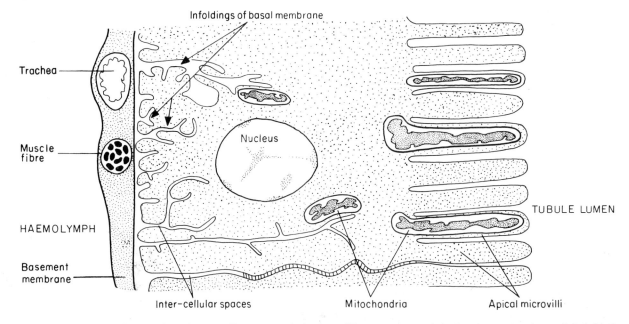

Fig. 2.6. Typical Malpighian tubule 'primary cell'. Many apical microvilli are present and the basement membrane is infolded extensively. Muscle fibres are not found in all species but when present, as in locusts, cockroaches and beetles, the tubules can undergo pronounced writhing and coiling movements.

unknown but it is likely that some reabsorption occurs from the tubule lumen (see also § 2.3.3). In some species the distal regions of the Malpighian tubules may form complex anatomical links with the rectal wall to form so-called *cryptonephridia* (§ 2.3.4).

2.3.2 Structural organization of the malpighian tubule

Both the basal and apical surfaces of the primary cell (Fig. 2.6) are highly infolded and associated with many mitochondria. This organization has led to the proposal that standing gradients are established within the narrow channels of the infoldings (§ 2.1). The distribution of the ion pumps responsible for ion transport and ultimately fluid secretion by the Malpighian tubules is still unknown. Recent evidence by Maddrell and colleagues suggests that the so-called 'potassium pump' on the apical membrane also has a high affinity for Na^+, indeed higher than for K^+. The pump will then pass both ions into the lumen and water will also pass from the cell into the lumen, so that the cell will tend to shrink. The large surface area of the basal membrane will facilitate water movement into the cell, this in turn will lower the intracellular concentrations of ions, and ions will tend to enter passively from the haemolymph. This flow of K^+ and the osmotic flow of water will flush excretory products and other components of the urine into the hind-gut.

2.3.3 The hind-gut and rectum

The selectivity of the insect excretory system resides primarily within the rectum. The rectal epithelium and specialized rectal pads reabsorb useful materials from the urine (as well as from mid-gut contents passing into the hind-gut) and pass these back into the haemolymph. Unwanted materials and those for which no specific reabsorptive mechanism exists are voided in the urine and faeces.

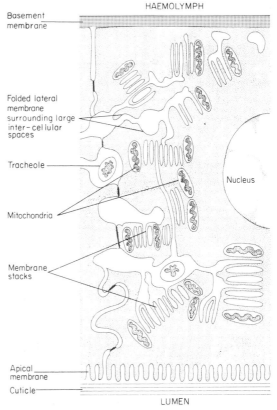

Fig. 2.8a. Diagram of the more important ultrastructural features of a rectal papilla cell. The large intercellular spaces communicate with the flattened stacks of intercellular membrane. These membrane stacks possess an active ATPase and are probably the site of active ion transport. The stacks are sandwiched between mitochondria. It is important to note that the basal membrane which is bathed in haemolymph is much reduced in surface area compared with the apical membrane facing the lumen of the rectum (From Berridge, M. J. (1970); see Fig. 2.2).

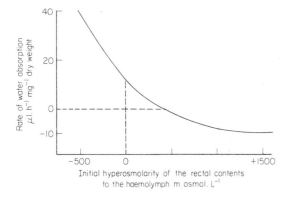

Fig. 2.7. Uptake of water from xylose solutions injected into the locust rectum. It is only at very high levels of osmolarity that water uptake is prevented (From Phillips, J. E. (1970) *Am. Zool.* **10**, 413-436).

Work on *Schistocerca* has provided much of our present knowledge of the physiology of the rectum. Phillips devised a technique in which the rectum is ligatured off from fluids passing from the mid-gut or the Malpighian tubules. Changes in the composition of various fluids introduced into the rectum (via the anus) can then be measured without contamination from other tissues, volume changes being monitored by changes in the concentration of radio-labelled albumen in the solutions. Locusts are able to void a urine hyper-osmotic to the haemolymph and can alter the composition of the urine markedly in relation to their diet. By using different concentrations of xylose (a sugar which is not absorbed by the rectum) to effect changes in OP, the relationship between water absorption and OP can be measured (Fig. 2.7). Water is absorbed rapidly when the rectal contents are iso-osmotic with the haemolymph and continues to be absorbed as the rectal concentration rises but stops when the rectal fluid reaches a concentration some three times that of the haemolymph (Fig. 2.7). This water movement is not caused by hydrostatic pressure and occurs without the net transport of solute into the haemolymph, because water uptake against a concentration gradient occurs even from pure xylose solutions. Similar observations have been made on *Calliphora* and *Periplaneta*.

The cuticular lining of the hind-gut is thought to act as a sieve to prevent the uptake of large molecular weight solutes. Water uptake in the hind-gut not only conserves water, but also facilitates the uptake of metabolites by increasing their concentration in the rectal lumen. It is also possible that excreted toxins could thus pass back into the haemolymph but this is presumably prevented by the low permeabillity of the cuticular lining. In *Schistocerca* this lining has water-filled pores 7 nm in diameter. Measurements with cuticle stripped off from the underlying epithelium show that it is 10-100 times more permeable to water than to K^+ or Na^+, and that large molecules such as disaccharides penetrate only slowly. Because these latter chemicals are required by the insect, it is likely that they are reabsorbed to some extent before they reach the rectum, perhaps by the Malpighian tubules (§ 2.3.1).

On the basis of the ultrastucture of the rectal pads

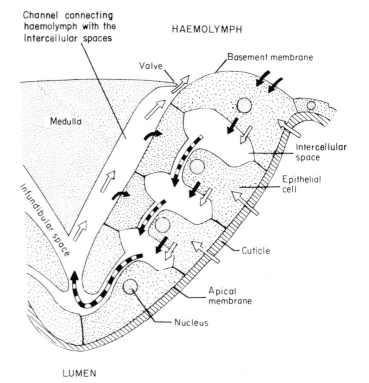

Fig. 2.8b. Schematic longitudinal view of an insect rectal papilla showing the route of fluid movement from the rectal lumen to the haemolymph. The large intercellular spaces connect, through a valve, with the haemolymph. Illustrated is the uptake of water (white arrows) across the papilla into the haemolymph in the absence of net uptake of solute. Solute (black arrows) is recycled by being returned into the rectal pads across the basement membrane; alternatively solute may be recruited from the haemo-lymph. This recycling of solute means that water is dragged into the epithelial cells from the rectal lumen (From Berridge, M. J. (1970); see Fig. 2.2).

(Fig. 2.8) it is proposed that active secretion of solutes (ions) occurs in the intercellular spaces and that this causes regions of high concentration into which water will flow passively. Other solutes will also flow into these spaces which will be effectively low in concentration for these solutes. The water will flow through the interconnecting spaces into the infundibular or subepithelial space, and when sufficient pressure is generated, the valve will open and water will pass into the haemolymph. This water should be deficient in ions if the ions are recycled as shown in Fig. 2.8. The folded stacks on the lateral membranes form the major sites for ion secretion. The stacks are sandwiched between mitochondria richly supplied with ATPase and thus possess the energy necessary for the functioning of ion pumps.

This interpretation is supported by the finding that the sizes of the intercellular spaces are related to the rates of water absorption. They are normally collapsed in starved flies but are large in starved flies whose rectal lumen has been injected with a hypo-osmotic solution. Only the latter type of flies has water available to satisfy the water conserving mechanisms.

2.3.4 Cryptonephridial systems

In many Coleoptera and Lepidoptera, the distal ends of the Malpighian tubules, which hang free in the haemolymph in other insects, are closely associated with the *rectum* to form a *cryptonephridial complex*. In *Tenebrio*, a pest of stored products, with no access to free water, the complex removes water from the faeces; the absorp-

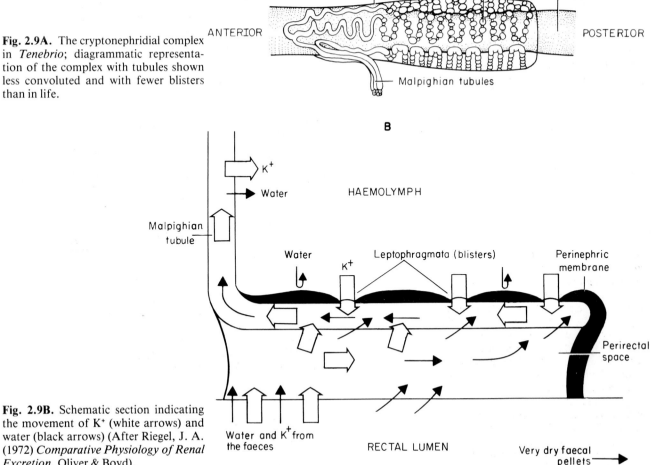

Fig. 2.9A. The cryptonephridial complex in *Tenebrio*; diagrammatic representation of the complex with tubules shown less convoluted and with fewer blisters than in life.

Fig. 2.9B. Schematic section indicating the movement of K⁺ (white arrows) and water (black arrows) (After Riegel, J. A. (1972) *Comparative Physiology of Renal Excretion.* Oliver & Boyd).

tive power is considerable, enabling *Tenebrio* to produce virtually dry faecal pellets. The organization of the complex is shown in Fig. 2.9. At their distal ends, the six Malpighian tubules are invested by a perinephric membrane and separated from the rectum by the perirectal space. Each tubule contains on its outer walls (haemolymph side) numerous scattered cells, which form blisters, the *leptophragmata,* on thin regions in the tubule wall and perinephric membrane, and separating the tubule lumen from the haemolymph. The rectal epithelium is similar in structure to that in other insects (Fig. 2.8) but the lateral membrane stacks are absent and numerous microtubules take their place.

The leptophragmata secrete K⁺ from the haemolymph into the tubule lumen, Cl⁻ following passively. The primary urine may be markedly hypertonic to the haemolymph (as high as 2M KCl) but water from the haemolymph is prevented from entering the tubule by the impermeability of the blisters and perinephric membrane. Water enters the tubule from the perirectal fluid, but the osmotic pressure of this is maintained high by the presence of a non-absorbable protein. A gradient of osmotic pressure in the perirectal fluid runs from anterior (low, left of Fig. 2.9**B**) to posterior (high), parallel to a quantitatively similar gradient in the tubules. The use of dyes suggest that flow in the perirectal space is in the opposite direction to that in the tubules, an arrangement reminiscent of *counter-current exchange* systems in other animals. The rectal epithelium pumps K⁺ into the perirectal fluid, and water is thereby taken up from the rectal lumen, especially at the most anterior region. The high osmotic pressure of this fluid clearly aids water movement from the rectum. The tubular fluid therefore becomes more dilute as it passes forward along the cryptonephridial system taking water from the perirectal fluid but, in dehydrated *Tenebrio,* the fluid leaving the complex is hyper-osmotic to the haemolymph and the free proximal portions of the tubules pump the excess K⁺ back into the haemolymph; water also passes into the haemolymph before the final urine enters the hind-gut. The cryptonephridial complex in Lepidoptera lacks leptophragmata and is probably concerned more with salt balance than water regulation, since caterpillars eat fresh plant material with a high water content.

2.4 WATER BALANCE

2.4.1 Terrestrial insects—hormones and water balance

Insects are well adapted to conserving water. This predisposition to water conservation means that special mechanisms have evolved to remove water excess. The insect has little control over loss of water through the cuticle, and most of the regulation of water balance is by the excretory and respiratory systems. In locusts, for example, the excretory system normally keeps the insect in positive water balance: urine passes into the rectum at a rate of 10-15 μl.h⁻¹ and this is less than the 17-20 μl.h⁻¹ basal rate of water uptake from the rectal lumen. However, some water will still be lost in the faeces and also through the cuticle and respiratory surfaces. Any deficit is made good by dietary intake. To promote water loss the insect releases a diuretic hormone (see below) and the volume of urine entering the gut is then in excess of the absorption capacity of the rectum. In times of water deprivation a minimal amount of fluid is secreted by the tubules and much of this is recovered by the rectum. The locust is also able to reduce respiratory water loss from 5 mg.h⁻¹ to 0.8 mg. h⁻¹ by reducing the tracheal ventilation rate (§ 1.1).

In the blood sucking bug, *Rhodnius,* which takes infrequent large meals, two neurosecretory hormones are released in response to feeding. One, released from axon terminals in the abdominal wall, is a *plasticization hormone* which increases the water content of the cuticle and makes it more stretchable to accommodate the meal. The other hormone is a *diuretic hormone* which is produced by twelve neurosecretory cells in the mesothoracic ganglion. The axon terminals do not form a specialized neurohaemal organ (§ 3.3.1), and the hormone is released from regions on the surface of the abdominal nerves. Cutting the ventral nerve cord prevents the controlled release of the diuretic hormone after feeding. Information from stretch receptors in the abdominal wall passes to a region of the neuropile of the thoracic ganglion which also receives branches from the neurosecretory cells. An integrative link presumably occurs here which accounts for the rapid response of the neurosecretory cells to abdominal distension. Ingestion of warm saline also induces rapid diuresis, so it is the distension of the abdomen *per se* which elicits hormone release. Sufficient hormone is released within 2 min of the onset of feeding to ensure maximum diuresis. *In vitro,* unstimulated tubules produce fluid at a rate of *c.* 0.1 nl.min^{-1}; the stimulated tubules at a rate of 60 nl. min^{-1}, i.e. 600 times faster. The diuretic hormone acts upon the Malpighian tubules to increase the volume of urine secreted without altering its composition. However, the hormone also promotes the reabsorption of K$^+$ from the proximal regions of the tubule (§ 2.3.1). Cessation of diuresis is achieved by the lack of release of hormone coupled with its rapid removal from the haemolymph by the Malpighian tubules which degrade it. The distension of the abdomen diminishes as diuresis proceeds but the stretch receptors are non-adapting and respond to the constant stretch stimulus even as it is reducing (§ 4.5.3). This ensures that hormone is released for as long as the blood-meal remains in the gut.

Diuretic hormones are also important in other insects. Locusts allowed access to fresh grass or lettuce will eat their own weight of food each day; this can result in a daily intake of 2000 μl of water. The blood volume of the insect is only 300-500 μl thus it is essential that the excess water is removed. The diuretic hormone in locusts is synthesized by the cerebral neurosecretory cells and released from the storage regions of the corpus cardiacum (§ 3.3.1). As in *Rhodnius,* the stimulus for release of the hormone is feeding; when previously starved locusts are allowed access to food, there is a marked increase in the secretory activity of the tubules due to the release of diuretic hormone (Table 2.2). The diuretic hormones of locusts, *Rhodnius* and *Glossina* have been purified partially, and seem to be small peptides.

There is uncertainty concerning the mode of action of diuretic hormones. It has been shown that the hormones act via a second messenger, cyclic AMP (cf. § 2.2.4). Addition of cAMP to the bathing medium markedly increases the rate of secretory activity of the tubules *in vitro*. In *Rhodnius,* a transitory increase (lasting 2-4 min) in intracellular levels of cAMP occurs in tubules stimulated by diuretic hormone, but no such increase occurs in locust tubules. These observations reveal little of the cellular events leading to increased fluid secretion. Solute pumps are likely to be activated by protein kinases which are themselves activated by cAMP. Such activation can occur either by increased

Experimental Group	No. of insects	Fluid secretion μl.h^{-1}
Starved	6	7.5
Starved then fed for 2.5 h	5	27.5
Starved injected with an homogenate of 0.5 pair of corpora cardiaca	5	14.2
Starved injected with 1.0 pair of corpora cardiaca	5	23.0

Table 2.2 Rates of fluid secretion by Malpighian tubules in intact locusts. The ileum was transected and a canula inserted to collect the primary urine from the Malpighian tubules. The mid-gut was ligatured off to prevent any mid-gut fluid passing into the ileum (from Mordue, W. (1972) *Gen. comp. Endocrinol. Suppl.* **3**). Feeding or injecting with diuretic hormone (corpus cardiacum cc extract) markedly increases fluid production.

concentrations of nucleotide or by its increased turnover.

Many target tissues which respond to peptide hormones, in both the invertebrates and vertebrates, are also stimulated by biogenic amines. In locusts, the Malpighian tubules increase fluid secretion in response to adrenalin, but not to 5-HT; *Rhodnius* tubules, on the other hand, do respond to 5-HT. In locusts the receptors for the peptide hormone and for adrenalin are separate. Tubules in which the adrenergic receptor has been blocked with phentolamine will still respond to diuretic hormone. In *Rhodnius* the diuretic hormone and 5-HT are presumed both to act at the same site. The aminergic system may be thought of as a relic of a previous dual control system; present evidence suggests that only peptides are now involved in the control of the Malpighian tubules. Many compounds, in addition to amines, promote increased fluid secretion, but it is not always clear whether this is diuresis *sensu stricto* or osmotic coupling of water transport to active transport or excretion of solutes.

The first effect of the diuretic hormone in *Rhodnius* is to change the electric potential across the tubule wall. During fluid production, chloride secretion is in excess of cation secretion (Fig. 2.10). The difference between the potential of the resting and stimulated tubule is not great, though the net flux of ions in the two states is very different. The time course for the transitory increase in intra-cellular levels of cAMP following stimulation

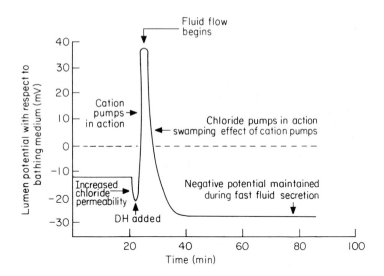

Fig. 2.10. Possible explanation for the effects of diuretic hormone (DH) upon the electropotential gradient in the Malpighian tubule of *Rhodnius* (From Maddrell, S. H. P. (1971). *Adv. Insect Physiol.* **8**, 200-331).

with diuretic hormone parallels these changes in potential closely.

It is possible that *anti-diuretic hormones* also exist but there is no conclusive evidence for their actions *in vivo*. In locusts, an anti-diuretic factor (hormone), from the glandular lobes of the corpus cardiacum increases water uptake *in vitro* from the rectal lumen. This action is opposite to the *in vitro* effect of the locust diuretic hormone. The 'anti-diuretic hormone' is without effect upon the Malpighian tubules and there is little good evidence, in any insects, for the existence of hormones which specifically reduce tubule secretion. In the absence of diuretic hormone the tubules secrete at a very low level, so there is probably no need for a hormone to turn them off.

2.4.2 Aquatic insects—ionic and osmotic regulation

Fig. 2.11 shows the relationships between the OP of the body fluids and the external medium in different insects. *Aedes aegypti* and *Culex pipiens* larvae live in fresh water and can regulate their haemolymph OP in low salinities, but as the OP of the environment increases (to c. 1.0% NaCl), osmo-regulation fails and they become *osmo-conformers*. *Aedes detritus,* which breeds in salt marshes, is an efficient *osmo-regulator*, maintaining nearly constant haemolymph OP in hypo-osmotic or hyper-osmotic media. *Chinoromus halophilus,* which breeds in brackish waters is able to regulate in fresh and brackish water, but only up to c. 2% NaCl. Caddis

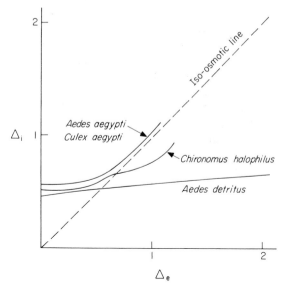

Fig. 2.11. The relationship between the osmotic pressure expressed as depression in freezing point, $\triangle$) of the haemolymph ($\triangle_i$)with that of the external medium ($\triangle_e$) in aquatic larvae.

fly larvae, however, can survive in more brackish waters than fresh water chironomids, are osmo-conformers, and tolerate haemolymph ionic concentrations some three times the normal value.

The larvae of some Diptera, and those of Ephemeroptera and Trichoptera, possess thin cuticular flaps which are sites of active ion uptake. Mosquito larvae have

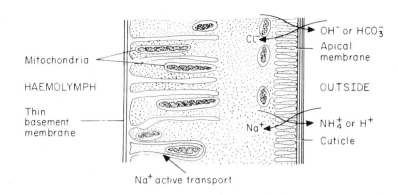

Fig. 2.12. Anal papilla cell of a larval mosquito. Extensive infoldings of both basal and apical membranes are present. Uptake of Na^+ and Cl^- occurs by separate exchange pumps situated on the apical membrane (From *Environmental Physiology* ed. J. G. Phillips, Blackwell Scientific Publications).

these as *anal papillae,* the size of which is related to the salinity of the environment, so that larger papillae are found in larvae inhabiting more dilute media. The increased surface area presumably facilitates ion uptake. This uptake is so efficient that if larvae are kept for a time in distilled water (which reduces the haemolymph ionic content equivalent to 0.05% NaCl) and then transferred to tap water, they readily restore their haemolymph to its normal level (equivalent to 0.3% NaCl) even though the ion content of tap water is only 0.006% NaCl. The cells of the anal papilla (Fig. 2.12) have many similarities to the secretory cells of the Malpighian tubules (Fig. 2.6). The absorptive mechanisms are most efficient when both Na^+ and Cl^- are taken up at the same time, though separate processes are involved. The uptake involves ion exchange: Na^+ ions are exchanged for NH_4^+ or H^+, and Cl^- for either HCO_3^- or OH^-. These exchanges involve ATPases and expenditure of energy.

Insects living in hyper-osmotic environments drink the external medium to obtain supplies of water lost through the cuticle. This water loss is minimized by the cuticular impermeability which is just as important to these insects as it is to terrestrial species. The regulatory mechanisms of the Malpighian tubules and rectum ensure that excess ions are excreted while as much water as possible is conserved. It is also possible that significant uptake of water occurs from the mid-gut lumen.

2.5 CUTICLE

The integument of the insect forms not only its main interface with the environment but has, perhaps, a more profound effect on its life than does the skin in any other animals. For example, the cuticle provides a rigid

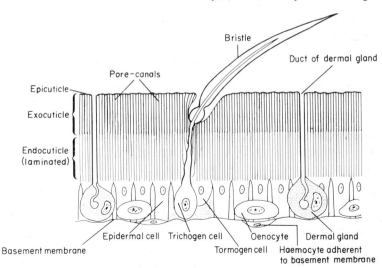

Fig. 2.13. Section of typical insect cuticle (From Wigglesworth, V. B. (1972) *Principles of Insect Physiology,* 7th Edn. Chapman & Hall).

exoskeleton but must allow articulation at the joints and, as the external covering of the body, it must resist abrasion and be waterproof. However, these properties restrict the possibility of increase in size and limit the form of the sense organs and appendages. In general, the cuticle consists of hardened sclerotized plates jointed together by thin unsclerotized strips; this arrangement provides rigidity with flexibility. Although there is great variety in the form and function of cuticle, its basic organization is common throughout the class (Fig. 2.13). The basement membrane (1-2 μm thick) is secreted by the haemocytes and is composed of neutral muco-polysaccharides. It separates the epidermis from the haemolymph and provides a mat over and through which run nerves and tracheoles.

The epidermis

The epidermis is a single-layered continuous sheet of cells beneath the cuticle. The density and number of cells varies throughout development and cell division occurs at times dictated by the hormonal milieu (§ 3.3.2). In some Diptera and Hymenoptera, the epidermal cells do not divide but increase in size as the larvae grow. The epidermis secretes the greater part of the cuticle and is also involved in wound repair. The differentiation of the epidermis determines not only the surface pattern-ing and shape of the insect but also its definitive size. Insects can increase in size only by periodically shedding the cuticle. The epidermis produces the *moulting fluid,* which contains proteinases and chitinases to digest the old endocuticle. The products of digestion are resorbed by the epidermis and recycled; resorption may also occur in periods of prolonged starvation. Many specialized gland cells and parts of cuticular sensillae are scattered among the normal epidermal cells. The cuticle is also the skeleton of the insect, and muscle attachments have to pass through the epidermis to be inserted into the endocuticle (§ 5.1.1).

Procuticle

The cuticle is divided over most of the body into three regions; endo-, exo- and epicuticle (Fig. 2.13). The exo- and endocuticle together are called the *procuticle* and consist primarily of a protein-chitin complex. *Chitin,* which can account for up to 60% of the dry weight of the cuticle, is a high molecular weight polysaccharide consisting mainly of N-acetyl glucosamine units joined by β-1,4 links that are very resistant to hydrolysis. The chitin chains are long and consist of several hundred units. The other major component of the cuticle, protein, is often complexed with the chitin by covalent linkages via aspartic acid and histidine residues. Cuticular proteins are often tanned, i.e. adjacent protein chains are cross-linked by O-quinones (p. 40). This process, called *sclerotization,* produces a tough hard inelastic material. In special regions of the cuticle the remarkable rubber-like protein *resilin* is found. Its polypeptide chains are organized into an isotropic three-dimensional mesh which is stabilized by covalent cross linkages. Resilin is readily deformed, but shows perfect elastic recovery; these properties make it especially useful in locomotion (§ 5.3.1). The chitin in the procuticle is deposited in a characteristic pattern of lamellae, usually in daily layers. As each layer is formed, the direction of the chitin fibrils rotates with respect to the previous lamella. This creates a helicoidal arrangement of the fibrils and accounts for the parabolic light patterns seen in some transverse sections. The organization of the cuticle in the *peritrophic membrane* is different; it exists as flat net-like sheets, and has a low chitin content. This affords some mechanical protection for the gut cells while allowing gut secretions and digestion products to pass through.

The homogeneous *endocuticle* is some 10-200 μm thick and is untanned. It can be reabsorbed and thus can be thought of as a food reserve. The *exocuticle,* the outer-most region of the procuticle, is tanned often darkly coloured and is indigestible. It is the exocuticle that forms the exuvium at moulting. In soft-bodied insects, the exocuticle is thin and scarcely distinguishable from the epicuticle, but in some beetles it is thick and comprises most of the procuticle.

The *epicuticle* (Fig. 2.13) is the thin complex outer layer secreted by the epidermis, dermal glands and oenocytes. It lacks chitin but contains proteins, lipids and polyphenols. Its outermost covering is often a cement layer, the composition of which is largely unknown. The cuticulin layer beneath this is *c.* 10 nm thick and is the first layer to be secreted during the deposition of new cuticle. Cuticulin is chemically complex and resistant to both acids and organic solvents; it probably consists of highly polymerized lipids. The major layer in the epicuticle is the protein epicuticle, a homogeneous layer about 1 μm thick and composed of lipid-protein complexes. When the epicuticle is first laid down on the surface of the epidermal cells prior to ecdysis, it is deeply folded. These folds are straightened out after ecdysis, when the insect inflates itself by swallowing air. The extent of this folding determines the size and shape of the insect in the succeeding instar.

Pore canals

Many processes take place at the surface of the cuticle, e.g. repair, wax secretion, release of tanning agents. These are dependent upon epidermal secretions which cross the cuticle to the outside of the insect via *pore canals*. These are originally cytoplasmic filaments extending from the epidermis, but may later become filled with cuticular material. The pores are less than 1 μm in diameter and are often twisted, following the helicoidal arrangement of the chitin fibres in the cuticular lamellae.

2.5.1 Cuticle permeability

In spite of its waxed and cemented layers, insect cuticle is partially permeable to water and polar compounds (§ 2.4.2), and rather more permeable to non-polar and lipophilic compounds. These permeability characteristics are of considerable importance in relation to the pene-tration of polar and non-polar insecticides (§ 4.9) and insect growth regulators (§ 3.6). Water loss from living insects increases more rapidly at temperatures above 30°C than below. Some of this increase is probably due to increased ventilatory movements at the higher temperatures, but other factors must also be important because dead insects with their spiracles occluded still show increased transpiration rates at high temperatures (Fig. 2.14). The marked change in rate of water loss occurs at what is called the *transition temperature*. Even slight abrasion of the epicuticle or removal of some of the surface wax by contact with absorbent but non-abrasive powders, abolishes the transition phenomenon and leads to high rates of water loss, even at low temperatures. The waterproofing of the cuticle in newly moulted insects is coincident with and dependent upon the deposition of the epicuticular lipids and waxes which are of utmost significance in restricting water loss through the cuticle. When extracted cuticular lipids are applied as a film to butterfly wings or water droplets it can be shown that these lipids are responsible for the waterproofing and the transition phenomena. The existence of transition temperatures is disputed by some workers (p. 29) who suggest that the increase in permeability is exponential and occurs because measurements were made in dry air. As the temperature is increased, vapour pressure gradients would increase also, and could

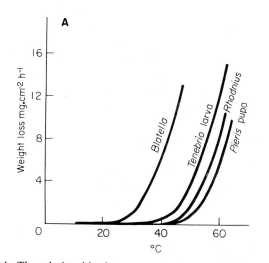

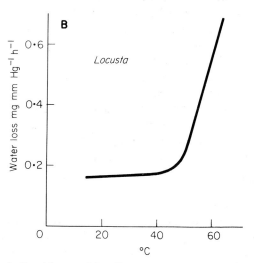

Fig. 2.14. The relationships between water loss and air temperature in. **A,** Dead insects. No adjustments are made for vapour pressure deficient or cuticular temperature. **B,** Water loss is adjusted for vapour pressure deficit—a transition phenomenon is still apparent.

account for the increased water loss. However, in some insects a transition temperature exists even when allowances are made for changes in vapour pressure (Fig. 2.14**B**). In addition, experiments in which cuticular temperature was measured still show the phenomenon, even though the cuticular temperature is much cooler than the air temperature becuase of evaporative cooling. It is not clear whether the high evaporative cooling above the transition temperature is of any significance in enabling the insect to withstand high temperatures. Insects such as *Tenebrio* and *Rhodnius* with hard cuticular waxes, often show relatively high transition temperatures and in general such species are more able to withstand desiccation than insects with low transition points. Once an insect has been heated above its transition point its cuticular transpiration is high even when the insect is returned to lower temperatures.

Physico-chemical basis for the transition phenomenon

Beament has suggested that a monolayer of organized lipid is present within the cuticular greases and waxes. In *Periplaneta,* if 95% of the cuticular wax is removed but the monolayer left intact, the permeability is increased three-fold rather than the expected twenty-fold. The monolayer is thus of major importance in waterproofing. The existence of this layer is disputed, however. Beament's hypothesis is that the monolayer lipids are orientated with their polar ends inwards and the hydrocarbon chains pointing outwards from the cuticulin. At low temperatures the molecules are arranged at an angle of 65° to the hydrophilic substrate which allows adjacent carbon chains to interdigitate and restrict water permeability. Above the transition temperature the hydrocarbon chains become perpendicular to the cuticulin, intermolecular channels open and water loss is facilitated.

Most evidence concerning the monolayer has come from *Periplaneta.* However, the cuticular lipids in this insect are mainly hydrocarbons lacking polar groups. Such compounds cannot form a close-packed monolayer. Many different lipids are found in the cuticle and it is likely that the temperature-induced changes in the packing of one lipid will affect the layer as a whole and create large intermolecular spaces. Cuticular lipids vary in different species and their differing compositions could account for the differing permeabilities and transition points.

2.5.2   Absorption of water vapour

Some insects can take up water from unsaturated atmospheres. This ability has been investigated in *Thermobia* and *Tenebrio*. *Tenebrio* larvae increase in weight, even though starved, if the relative humidity is more than 88%; *Thermobia* can extract water from air at 45% r.h. and 21°C. Desiccated *Thermobia (weighing 30 mg) can absorb water at a rate of 5 μg.min^{-1},* but uptake stops once the normal body water content is regained. The process is thus under control. This uptake does not occur through the cuticle in general, as was once thought, but is restricted to the hind-gut, uptake being prevented completely by occlusion of the anus. The posterior region of the rectum forms a chamber which opens to the outside through valves. These valves are closed in a fully hydrated insect but open and close every 1-2 s if a dehydrated insect is exposed to humidities of more than 45% r.h. This ventilation rate can be shown to provide sufficient water in the rectum to allow the measured absorption rate. The diffusion of water vapour between the air and rectal epithelium is aided by the ventilation which prevents the establishment of an equilibrium between the absorbing surface and the air. In *Tenebrio* the site of uptake of water vapour is also the rectum; this can be closed off from the air by anal valves if the humidity falls below 88%.

It is not clear how these absorptive mechanisms work. In *Thermobia* the organization of the rectal epithelium is elaborate and associated with specialized transport mechanisms, but in *Tenebrio* the organization is less complex. To remove water from air at 88% r.h. by solute coupling would require solutions of very high OP (for example a solution of saturated NaCl is in equilibrium with 75% r.h.). A compound such as glycerol, in which water is soluble, may be able to generate sufficient absorptive power. However, even if compounds such as this, or the protein present in the perirectal space in *Tenebrio* (§ 2.3.4), are involved, the problem remains of how this compound would release its water to the haemolymph.

Further reading

Berridge M. J. & Oschman J. L. (1972) *Transporting Epithelia.* Academic Press.

Gupta B. L., Moreton R. B., Oschman J. L. & Wall B. J. (Eds.) (1977) *Transport of Ions and Water in Animals.* Academic Press. (Selected Chapters).

Maddrell S. H. P. (1971) The mechanisms of insect excretory systems. *Adv. Insect Physiol.* **8**, 200-331.

Neville A. C. (Ed.) (1970) Insect ultrastructure. *Symp. R. ent. Soc.,* **8**.

Chapter 3
Growth and Development

The life cycle of an organism consists of a series of progressive changes which begin at fertilization and end shortly after death; they consist of periods of growth and replication during which a single cell, the egg, becomes an adult with millions of cells. Collectively these changes are known as development. This chapter examines the important components of growth, morphogenesis and sexual maturation.

Pterygote insects are not unique in showing in their post-embryonic life an almost complete change of body form or metamorphosis, but the changes are often dramatic and are under endocrine control. The study of insect development has provided an obvious and exciting challenge to physiologists.

3.1 GROWTH

The term growth has several meanings. It may be an increase in cell number, cytoplasmic or nuclear weight or volume, or in some constituent of protoplasm that is a constant proportion of the whole (for example, nitrogen or protein); so an animal may grow in one sense, but not in another, according to the particular measure employed. Insect growth is often described as discontinuous because the semi-rigid exoskeleton allows dramatic increases in linear dimensions only at a moult. However, growth in terms of weight or DNA content, for example, is almost continuous except when brief periods of reduced or zero growth occur. The visible expression of growth requires the insect to moult, at least in the juvenile stages, and because moulting is under endocrine control (§ 3.3.2) the hormones concerned with juvenile development have sometimes been linked with the control of growth. However, it is important to realize that insects do not possess a general growth hormone of the type that occurs in other animals. Instead, growth appears to be a property of individual cells and may be controlled locally.

3.2 MORPHOGENESIS

How differentiation occurs so that some cells become epiderm while others form muscles or nerves, and how genetic information is translated to form three-dimensional structures are largely unknown. These problems have been studied, however, particularly in relation to the control of cuticular patterns. Each epidermal cell secretes cuticle, either as a relatively flat plane or as specialized structures such as hairs, bristles, scales etc. (§ 2.5). The patterns within the cuticle are therefore essentially of a two-dimensional nature, and this simplifies to some extent the analysis of pattern. A number of theories have been proposed to explain *pattern formation* in insect cuticle but direct evidence is often lacking. Nevertheless, it is clear that epidermal cells receive positional information. The most widely accepted theory envisages that this information is provided by *gradients* in each segment. At a simple level we can imagine these as running antero-posteriorly and laterally (left to right). There is good evidence that a gradient along the long axis of each segment is initiated or maintained by the intersegmental membranes. Thus the position of any one cell can be specified by its coordinates along these axes. Although no chemical has been extracted or identified, it is supposed that these gradients are of the concentration of a diffusable molecule. Inherent in this hypothesis is the necessity for individual epidermal cells to recognize their position and to make an appropriate response to the information. It is thought that the positioning (spacing out) and orientation of bristles and scales, etc. could also be controlled by such diffusible molecules.

Experiments on leg regeneration in the cockroach, *Leucophaea,* suggest that the gradients which exist in each leg segment (except the trochanter) are responsible for the control of local growth and regeneration in these segments (Fig. 3.1). When cells find themselves adjacent to other cells of a different value in the gradient,

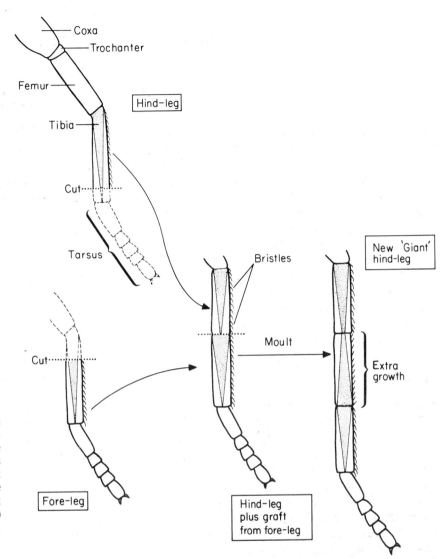

Fig. 3.1. A schematic representation of a leg regeneration experiment in the cockroach. The shaded area represents the hypothetical gradient along the long axis of the tibia. Note the extra growth produced by the discontinuity in the gradient, and the reversal of the gradient in the new tissue (From Bohn H. (1976) In: *Insect Development* Ed. P. A. Lawrence, *Symp. R. ent. Soc., Lond.,* **8**, 170-185).

growth occurs to restore the missing values *between* the two existing levels. Missing values of higher points in the gradient cannot, however, be formed. The amount of regenerative growth will therefore depend on the differences in gradient values. In the experiment illustrated in Fig. 3.1, because the gradient is reversed locally (in the regenerated tissue), the orientation of bristles is also reversed in the region of new growth. One puzzling feature of such experiments and those involving patches of cuticle which have been cut out, rotated through 180°, and replaced, is that the epidermal

cells appear to 'remember' their previous position in the gradient for long periods; for several moults in some instances. In other words, the gradient influence of the 'host' cuticle into which the transplant was made does not quickly reverse that of the graft. It is difficult to understand why the intersegmental membrane should need continually to signal the gradient when epidermal cells remember their positional information in this way.

Recently, it has been suggested that the insect body is subdivided into *compartments* whose development is largely autonomous. The existence of compartments is suggested by results from a variety of experiments. In the bug *Oncopeltus,* X-irradiation of eggs can result in the production of coloured patches of cuticle in the larvae. The distribution of these patches, each representing a clone (cells all originating from a single progenitor cell), suggests that each body segment is divided into quadrants; the cells in each clone of pigmented cells never cross a boundary between segments or adjacent quadrants (compartments). The importance of the compartment hypothesis may be widespread, since the developmental fate of the differently determined cells within a compartment may be under the control of a single regulator gene. Thus in *Drosophila,* a boundary dividing the wing into anterior and posterior compartments has been identified. There is also a mutation ('bithorax') that is responsible for transforming the anterior compartment of the metathoracic appendage into a wing instead of a normal haltere. This suggests that this compartment is under the control of a single regulator gene whose wildtype function is responsible for determining the development of the whole compartment as anterior haltere. Compartments could therefore be viewed as units for the control of morphogenesis and, at a broader level, for evolution.

3.3 ENDOCRINE CONTROL OF DEVELOPMENT

As discussed in § 3.2, much of differentiation is a property of individual cells, though it may be initiated by hormonal signals. However, many aspects of later development in larvae and adults are controlled by hormones. The endocrine glands and the morphogenetic actions of their hormonal secretions are considered in the following sections.

3.3.1 Sources of hormones

Neurosecretory cells

A number of modified neurones called neurosecretory cells (§ 4.8) are scattered throughout the nervous system (see Fig. 3.2) and are dominant in the control of insect development. They act to link the central nervous system, which monitors environmental information, with epithelial endocrine glands whose secretions control tissue differentiation. The predominant secretory function of neurosecretory cells is to provide long-

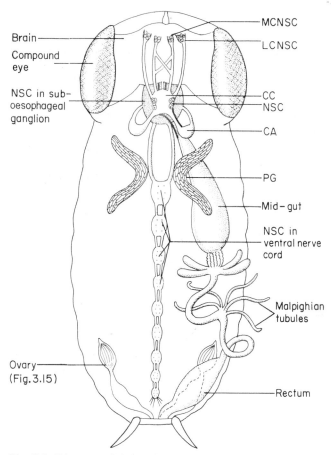

Fig. 3.2. Diagram of the major endocrine centres in a female insect. MCNSC and LCNSC are medial and lateral cerebral neurosecretory cells in the pars intercerebralis; CC, corpus cardiacum; CA, corpus allatum; PG, protharacic gland; NSC, neurosecretory cells (See also Fig. 4.2, p. 55.) (After Novak, V. J. A. (1975) *Insect Hormones.* Methuen).

distance communication with their target organ(s). Neurosecretory cells are found throughout the nervous system but occur in major groups in the *pars intercerebralis* of the brain (Fig. 3.2). The majority of the axons from the median groups cross over and leave the back of the brain via paired composite nerve tracts to their contralateral *corpus cardiacum;* most of the axons from the lateral groups innervate the ipsilateral corpus cardiacum (Fig. 3.2). Some of these neurosecretory axons pass through the paired corpora cardiaca to reach other tissues or endocrine glands but most terminate in the corpora cardiaca. The corpora cardiaca, as part of the stomatogastric nervous system, arise embryologically as ingrowths of the dorsal wall of the stomodaeum. They thus consist of nerve cells which, in most insects, take the form of neurosecretory cells with modified short stumpy axons or, as in the locust, with no easily identifiable axons. We have discussed already the hyperglycaemic (§ 1.4.1) and adipokinetic (§ 1.4.3) hormones produced by such intrinsic neurosecretory cells of the corpora cardiaca. These glands present therefore an intriguing parallel in structure with the vertebrate pituitary gland, since the adenohypophysis also arises from an ingrowth of the roof of the endodermal fore-gut (though in insects the stomodaeum is ectodermal). Whether this parallelism extends to details of function is unknown. In the corpora cardiaca, the axonal endings of the cerebral neurosecretory cells may form a close association with the intrinsic neurosecretory cells, or may, as in locusts and crickets, remain more or less separate from them. In either case the different cells are closely associated with the heart and form neurohaemal organs. Other neurosecretory cells are found in the ganglia of the ventral nerve cord (Fig. 3.2), associated with segmental neurohaemal organs, and occasionally in peripheral nerves in the abdominal nerve net.

Corpora allata

The corpora allata are always found associated with the corpora cardiaca but are true epithelial glands, arising embryologically from buds of ectoderm between the mandibular and maxillary segments. The corpora allata in bugs and more specialized Diptera often fuse to form a single median gland. The corpora allata secrete juvenile hormone but this may be different in chemical structure in different insects or even in the same species at different times (§ 3.3.5).

Prothoracic glands

The prothoracic glands develop in close association with the salivary glands as ingrowths of the ectoderm in the second maxillary segment. In primitive species, such as locusts, they remain as compact bodies in the head but in other insects they move backwards as loose chains of cells (Fig. 3.2). In the higher Diptera, they unite dorsally with the corpus allatum and ventrally with the corpus cardiacum to form a composite *ring gland*. The pro-

thoracic glands secrete ecdysone (§ 3.3.3) in larvae, but in the adult pterygote insect degenerate shortly after the imaginal moult. In Apterygotes, which alternately moult and reproduce throughout adult life, the glands persist and continue to secrete ecdysone.

3.3.2 Hormones and moulting

In insects, a univeral mechanism exists for the regulation of moulting. This involves the brain neurosecretory cells, the corpora cardiaca and the prothoracic glands. When the cerebral neurosecretory cells are removed early in the instar, moulting is prevented. Re-implantation of brains or parts containing the neurosecretory cells restores moulting, though a delay in moulting often occurs in these re-implanted insects while sites for the release of neurosecretions are regenerated. Evidently the cerebral neurosecretory system is essential for moulting. The involvement of the prothoracic glands in moulting has been established by the use of ligatures tied at different levels along the larval body. If a ligature is applied between the thorax and abdomen early in the instar, only the regions anterior to the ligature will moult, i.e. that part containing the prothoracic glands. Thus the prothoracic glands are also necessary for moulting. The interrelationships between the cerebral neurosecretory cells and the prothoracic glands are discussed below.

Control of moulting hormone production

The endocrine control of moulting has been established in many species but is best known from the work of Wigglesworth on *Rhodnius*. This blood-sucking bug feeds once during each larval instar and moults a fixed time after feeding. It is the size of the blood-meal and the degree of abdominal distension which is critical in activating the moulting process. Nutrition alone is an insufficient stimulus because if the insect is allowed to take many small meals (equivalent in total to one large meal) moulting is not initiated. Distension of the abdomen by a large blood-meal is monitored by segmental stretch receptors whose input to the CNS elicits the release of brain hormone from the cerebral neurosecretory cells. Cutting the nerve cord after a blood-meal prevents the signals from the stretch receptors reaching the brain; brain hormone is then not released and moulting does not occur. In insects which feed

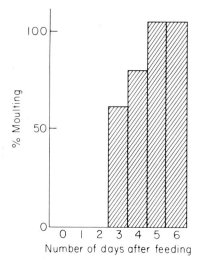

Fig. 3.3. The effect of decapitation at different days after feeding upon moulting in 2nd instar larvae of *Rhodnius*. Under these conditions the critical period (see text) ends 5-6 days after feeding.

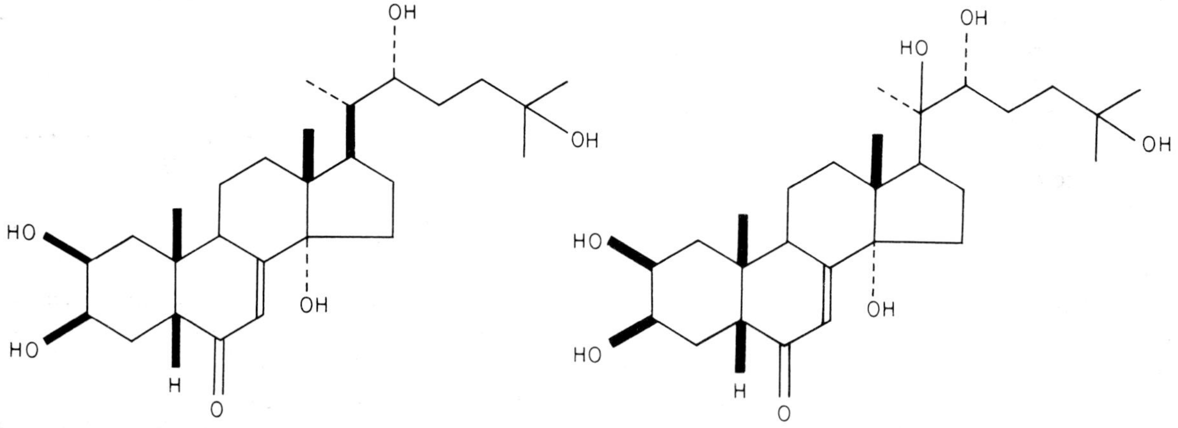

produce the moulting hormone. In many insects brain hormone does not act simply as a trigger; the prothoracic glands have to be exposed to it for long periods (Fig. 3.3). The time taken for their full activation is called the *critical period.* Removal of the cerebral neurosecretory cells (and therefore brain hormone) after the critical period does not prevent moulting because the prothoracic glands now function independently. The chemical identity of brain hormone is uncertain but it may be a glycoprotein of 20 000 molecular weight.

3.3.3   Moulting hormones (ecdysteroids)

The term *ecdysteroid* here refers to any steroid with moult-promoting activity. In other texts the term ecdysone is often used as a generic term for moulting hormone but a more specific terminology is to be preferred; ecdysone is a specific ecdysteroid (Fig. 3.4). During development, the cuticle separates from the epidermis (*apolysis*) before the epidermal cells differen-

ecdysone (α-ecdysone)   ecdysterone (β-ecdysone)

Fig. 3.4. Structures of the two most important ecdysteroids in insects.

repeatedly or continuously, feeding stimuli are also important in the activation of moulting. Both the quantity and quality of the diet may be important.

The *brain hormone* produced by the cerebral neurosecretory cells and released from the corpora cardiaca can be called ecdysiotropin, prothoracotropic hormone, or activation hormone because it acts as a tropic hormone which stimulates the prothoracic glands to

tiate, divide and deposit the new cuticle; when the new cuticle has been deposited, the old cuticle must be shed (*ecdysis*) so that the insect can increase in size. Ecdysteroids produced by the prothoracic glands control both apolysis and ecdysis (Fig. 3.5).

Ecdysteroids are not species specific and are all related to cholesterol. The two most important in insects are *ecdysone* (α-ecdysone) and *ecdysterone* (β-ecdysone);

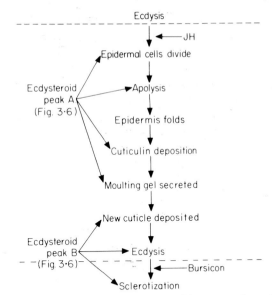

Fig. 3.5. Scheme for the involvement of hormones in cuticular development.

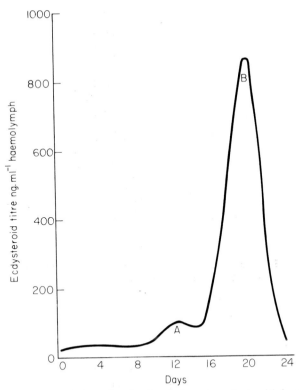

Fig. 3.6. Variations in the haemolymph ecdysteroid levels during the last larval instar of the dragonfly *Aeshna*. Two major peaks A and B occur (cf. Fig. 3.5.).

see Fig. 3.4. Ecdysterone is identical with crustecdysone—the moulting hormone of Crustacea. Ecdysteroids differ somewhat from vertebrate steroid hormones in that they possess many hydroxyl groups making them polar and very water soluble. Insects are unable to synthesize the steroid nucleus from acetate or mevalonate and rely upon dietary cholesterol or those phytosterols which can be converted into cholesterol. Both ecdysone and ecdysterone are found in insects but in general the latter predominates. It is uncertain which of them affects the target tissues to elicit moulting. ^{3}H-ecdysone injected into insects is hydroxylated rapidly to ^{3}H-ecdysterone so it appears that ecdysone may be a prohormone from which the active hormone, ecdysterone, is produced. Prothoracic glands taken from an appropriate stage in the instar will, in culture, produce ecdysone from cholesterol bound to protein. Thus it is now accepted that ecdysone is released from the prothoracic glands. But is this the hormone that is taken up by receptors on the target tissues, or is it converted to ecdysterone first, or does each steroid have its own role to play?

The levels of hormone shown in Fig. 3.6 were estimated using a sensitive radio-immunoassay procedure. This, and specialized gas and liquid chromatographic techniques, enable the different amounts of ecdysone and ecdysterone

present during development to be estimated, revealing that there are two peaks of ecdysteroid in the haemolymph during each instar. The existence of the larger peak is correlated with the deposition of the new cuticle and the events leading to ecdysis. The earlier, smaller peak, initiates apolysis and subsequent events (Fig. 3.5). Prior to the development of these chemical methods, *Calliphora* and *Musca* bioassays were used to estimate ecdysteroid levels. In these, last instar larvae are ligatured prior to the critical period so that the secretions of the prothoracic gland (part of the ring gland) are restricted to the anterior of the insect. The posterior half of the larva is then injected with hormone extract. The amount of extract necessary to induce puparium formation (see below) in 50% of the ligated abdomens is determined. This amount is known as a '*Calliphora* unit' and is equivalent to 4 ng of ecdysone or ecdysterone. It can thus be calculated how many *Calliphora* units are present in the extract.

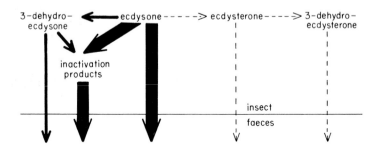

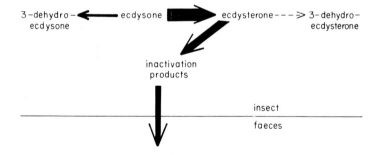

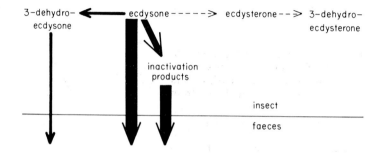

Fig. 3.7. Metabolism of radiolabelled ecdysone injected into the haemolymph of larvae and adults of *Locusta.* The relative importance of the pathways is indicated by the thickness of the arrows (From Hoffmann, J. A. *et al.,* (1974) *Gen. comp. Endocr.* **22**, 90-97.).

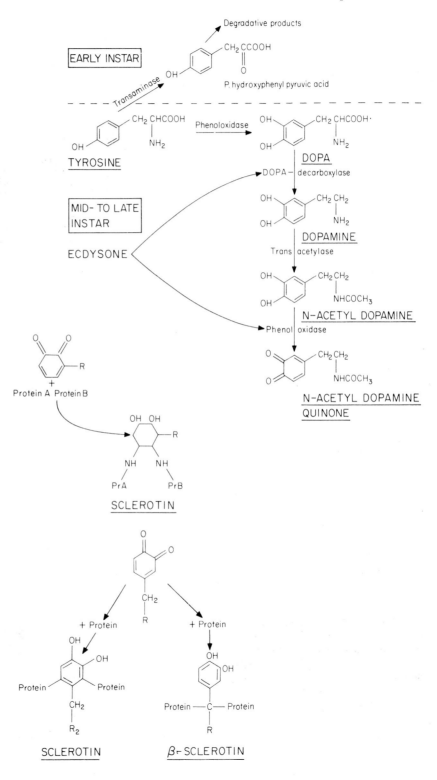

Fig. 3.8. Tryosine metabolism in *Calliphora*. Ecdysone regulates the production of DOPA-decarboxylase and switches tyrosine metabolism from transamination to quinone formation. Ecdysone may also activate the phenoloxidase involved in quinone formation. Sclerotin is formed by a tanning reaction between the quinone and proteins; a variety of mechanisms have been proposed.

In vertebrates, many steroid hormones are lipoidal, relatively insoluble in blood, and have to be transported attached to specific carrier proteins. In insects, however, this is generally not necessary because insect steroid hormones are water soluble.

In *Locusta,* the inactivation of ecdysteroids has been examined in detail; the major inactivation products are sulphate and, to a lesser extent, glycoside conjugates (Fig. 3.7). The excretion and hydroxylation of radio-labelled ecdysone injected into locusts varies markedly during the instar and forms part of an effective system for regulating the half-lives and therefore the titres of circulating ecdysteroids.

Mode of action of ecdysteroids

In vertebrates, the target tissues for steroid hormones contain cytoplasmic protein receptors that are absent from non-target tissues. The hormone penetrates the cell membrane, binds to cytoplasmic receptors and the steroid receptor complex, and then enters the nucleus to activate specific genes. In insects, steroid hormones also activate genes but the precise mechanism is unclear because target tissue receptors for ecdysteroids have not been investigated.

Sclerotization

The action of ecdysteroids on the formation of the new cuticle and the absorption of the old endocuticle has been little studied. Most work has concentrated on the role of ecdysteroids in cuticular sclerotization, especially in the blowfly puparium by Karlson and co-workers. In cyclorraphous Diptera, the pupa develops within a *puparium* formed by the retention and tanning of the last larval skin. Sclerotization occurs by interactions between cuticular proteins and the quinone derived from N-acetyl dopamine (Fig. 3.8). In the scheme proposed by Karlson the formation of N-acetyl dopamine from di-hydroxy phenyl alanine (DOPA), is a rate-limiting step. Early in the instar transamination of tyrosine predominates but in the mid- to late-instar, ecdysteroids switch the metabolism of tyrosine to hydroxylation and decarboxylation. DOPA-decarboxylase activity in the epidermis increases in parallel with the titre of ecdysteroid. In addition, enzyme activity increases in abdomens of ligated larvae within 10 h of ecdysone injection, but the response can be prevented by inhibitors of RNA synthesis.

Newly formed mRNA synthesized in response to ecdysone is therefore necessary for the *de novo* synthesis of DOPA-decarboxylase. It is possible to extract a mRNA coded for DOPA-decarboxylase from epidermal cells exposed to ecdysone.

In the puparium, therefore, ecdysone initiates tanning. However, during larva-to-larva moults the ecdysone present, which causes the moult, does not induce the formation of DOPA-decarboxylase, and the thin cuticle of the maggots is not sclerotized. In adult flies the cuticle is sclerotized, but in the pupa-to-adult transformation the enzyme is active when ecdysteroids are scarcely detectable. Thus, moulting hormone does not always initiate the synthesis of DOPA-decarboxylase, and at certain times enzyme activity increases in the absence of large amounts of hormone. It is possible that ecdysone merely initiates a programme of development appropriate to the state of differentiation of the target tissue. For example, in *Musca autumnalis* the hardening of the puparium is also regulated by ecdysone, but here the hormone controls calcium deposition.

Chromosome puffs

The action of ecdysteroids upon chromosome puffs has also been studied. In Diptera, puffs occur in the *polytene chromosomes* of tissues which grow by increasing in cell size rather than by mitotic division. This produces chromosomes up to 100 times larger than normal (i.e. 1 mm in length and 50 μm thick). In tissues which are only one cell thick, e.g. salivary glands and Malpighian tubules, these chromosomes are easily observed with the light microscope. Each chromosome possesses bands of DNA and histones; each band is thought to be a group of genes. During each instar certain bands puff at characteristic times. Such swellings may be areas of derepressed genes underoing intense mRNA synthesis (Fig. 3.9); actinomycin D, which blocks DNA-dependent RNA synthesis abolishes puffing.

Puffs appear at and for specific times in each instar and are related to particular events. The patterns vary from tissue to tissue and from instar to instar. For example, in *Drosophila* it is possible to relate the appearance of one set of puffs with the production of a cement to attach the pupa to the substrate. As little as 2 ng of ecdysone injected early in the last instar larva of *Chironomus* causes puffs which would normally appear just

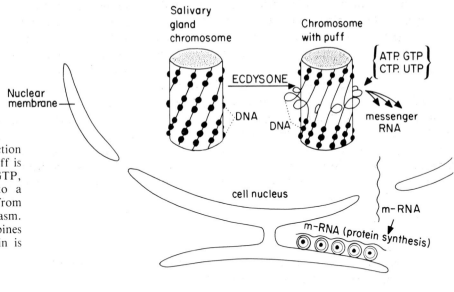

Fig. 3.9A. General scheme for the action of ecdysteroid. A chromosome puff is formed, and nucleotides (ATP, GTP, CTP, UTP) are incorporated into a specific mRNA. This is released from the puff and passes into the cytoplasm. The newly formed mRNA combines with ribosomes, and a new protein is produced.

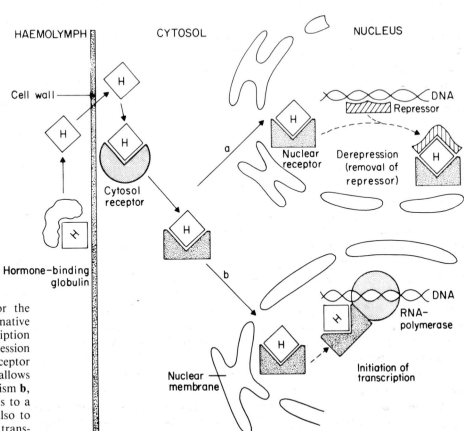

Fig. 3.9B. Proposed schemes for the action of ecdysteroids (H). Alternative mechanisms for inducing transcription are shown. In mechanism **a**, derepression is involved and the steroid-receptor complex removes a repressor and allows transcription to begin. In mechanism **b**, the steroid-receptor complex binds to a special region of the DNA and also to RNA polymerase. This initiates transcription. (After Karlson.)

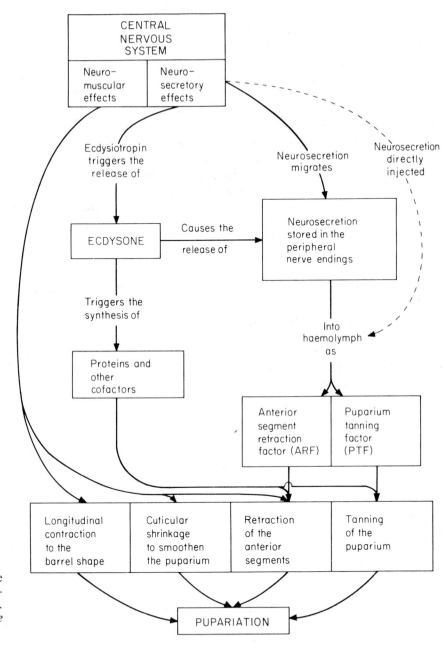

Fig. 3.10. A hypothetical scheme for the control of puparium formation in *Sarcophaga*. (From Sivasbrumanian P. et al., (1974) *Biol. Bull Wood's Hole* **147**, 163-185).

prior to the larval-pupal moult when the endogenous ecdysteroid titre is high. Two puffs appear within 15 min of the injection and others within 5-72 h. Ecdysone and ecdysterone initiate different puffing patterns and this may indicate specific roles for the two steroids. It must be emphasized that not all puffs depend upon ecdysone for their appearance and some pupal puffs occur only in its absence.

These observations do not show unequivocally the precise mechanism of action of the ecdysteroids. The hormones may act directly upon the genes (Fig. 3.9) or indirectly by affecting the permeability of the nuclear membrane to ions. An increased flux of K$^+$ into the nucleus could induce the puffing; the hormone need not enter the nucleus.

In addition to ecdysone two other hormones are involved in pupariation. A scheme for their actions is shown in Fig. 3.10. The release of two cerebral neuro-secretions ARF (anterior segment retraction factor) and PTF (puparium tanning factor) from peripheral nerve endings is controlled by ecdysone. PTF is not involved in the production of DOPA-decarboxylase but regulates the synthesis of enzyme (at the transcriptional level) necessary for the hydroxylation of tyrosine. Both neuro-hormones are proteins with molecular weights of 200 000 (ARF) and 300 000 (PTF).

3.3.4 Bursicon

Tanning of the exocuticle and post-moult deposition of the endocuticle in many larval and adult insects is controlled by a neurosecretion called *bursicon* (Fig. 3.5). In Diptera, the hormone is produced by the brain neuro-secretory cells and released from the thoracic ganglia, but in other insects it is thought to be released by the terminal abdominal ganglion. Bursicon is a protein of 40 000 MWt and is not species specific. Its action in tanning is to allow the formation of DOPA from hydroxylation of tyrosine. Tyrosine is present in the haemolymph of the insect but the hydroxylases are restricted to the insides of haemocytes. Bursicon increases the permeability of the haemocytes to tyrosine, and thus permits the substrate and enzyme to react. (The blood of many insects darkens on exposure to air because the haemocytes degenerate, thus allowing the formation of DOPA which when further oxidized forms melanins.) In many insects hydroxylation of tyrosine is an important rate limiting step in the sequence of events leading to tanning. It has been suggested that bursicon is responsible for plasticization of newly moulted cuticle, allowing its full extension before sclerotization. It is not clear why insects possess two mechanisms to control tanning, one controlled by ecdysone steroids and the other by bursicon. In species with aquatic stages, and in species which develop beneath a substrate or in confined spaces, a delay in tanning, relative to ecdysis, may be advantageous in that it allows the newly emerged insect to reach the surface before hardening begins. This will be especially true for the expansion of the wings. Thus while ecdy-

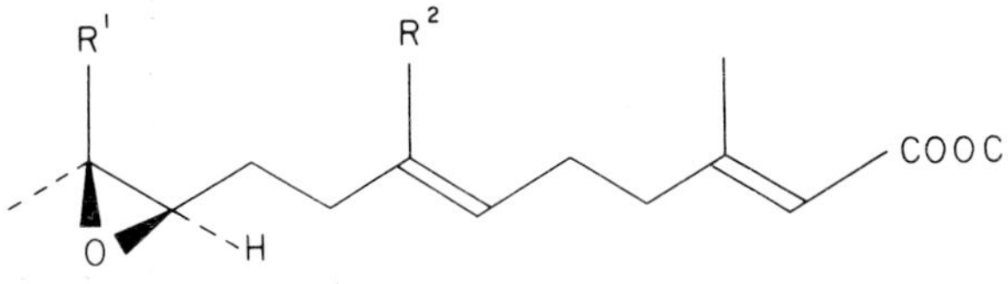

JH$-$I : R^1 = R^2 = C$_2$H$_5$
JH$-$II : R^1 = C$_2$H$_5$, R^2 = CH$_3$
JH$-$III : R^1 = R^2 = CH$_3$

Fig. 3.11. Structures of insect juvenile hormones.

steroids initiate ecdysis and perhaps the formation of DOPA-decarboxylase, in most insects tanning occurs only when bursicon stimulates the formation of DOPA.

3.3.5 Juvenile hormones

Secretions from the corpora allata (*juvenile hormones*) have two major roles: the control of metamorphosis and regulation of reproductive development. Juvenile hormone (JH) is one or more of a mixture of three terpenoids (Fig. 3.11). The hormones are referred to usually as JH-I (C-18 juvenile hormone), JH-II (C-17 juvenile hormone) and JH-III (C-16 juvenile hormone). The hormones are called 'juvenile', but it must be stressed that their actions are not restricted to the juvenile stages.

The isolation and characterization of JH has allowed estimates to be made of the presence of the three hormones in different insect groups. In most instances, only hormones present in adult insects have been examined and only JH-III has been detected. However, in the cockroach, *Nauphoeta,* all three hormones occur in larvae and adult females. In larvae 50% of the total JH present is JH-III, but in the adults 95% is. Similarly in *Manduca,* the adult female contains only JH-III but the larvae also possess JH-I which predominates. It has been suggested that the different hormones or ratios of them are characteristic of larval or adult stages.

Juvenile hormones and metamorphosis

Metamorphosis is controlled by juvenile hormone and its effects are considered here using *Rhodnius* as an example. Moulting is prevented in all stages by decapitation before the critical period but decapitation during the critical period allows some insects to moult (Fig. 3.3). Examina-

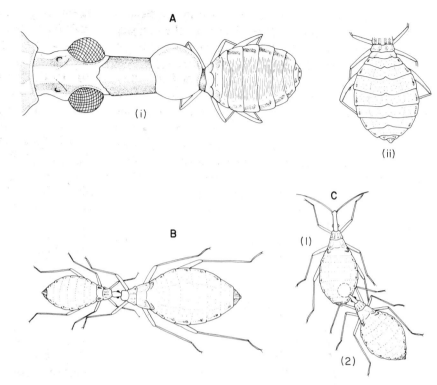

Fig. 3.12. A. (i) Production of a precocious 'adult' *Rhodnius* from a first instar by parabiosis to a moulting fifth (last) instar. (ii) Normal second instar larva for comparison (see text for further details). **B.** Parabiosis between a fourth instar, with head intact (except for the extreme tip), and a decapitated fifth instar larva. At moulting the fourth instar develops normally to the fifth stage; the fifth stage does not metamorphose but retains larval characters. **C.** Parabiosus between two fourth instars; if larva-1 has fed 24 h previously and larva-2 7 days previously, the moult results in a normal 5th instar from larva-2 but larva-1 moults into a form intermediate between the fourth and fifth stage. JH is present in larva-2 and larva-1 receives the hormone too early in the moulting process (see text for details) (After Wigglesworth, V. B. (1940 & 1952) *J. exp. Biol.* **17**, 201-222, and *J. exp. Biol.* **29**, 620-631).

tion of early instars shows that the cuticle formed in these latter insects has undergone precocious metamorphosis. The deposited cuticle shows some adult characters, such as partial differentiation of the wings and genitalia. This effect diminishes through the critical period and by its end all decapitated insects which moult show no metamorphosis.

In his classical parabiosis experiments (Fig. 3.12) Wigglesworth showed that larval characters are maintained and metamorphosis is inhibited by juvenile hormone:

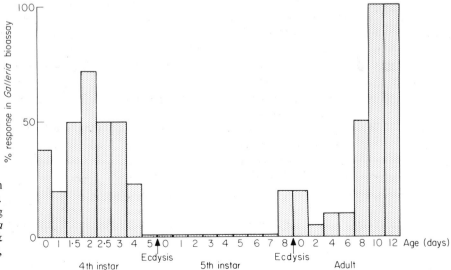

Fig. 3.13. Variations in the haemolymph titre of JH in larval and adult *Locusta*. Note the virtual absence of JH during the last (5th) larval instar. For *Galleria* assay see p. 46 (After Johnson, R. A. & Hill, L. (1973) *J. Insect Physiol.* **19**, 1921-1932 and 2459-2467).

the precocious metamorphosis observed in the decapitation experiments (Fig. 3.3) resulted from the removal of the corpus allatum. In the last stage larva, JH is not secreted and metamorphosis occurs; if a first stage larva is decapitated immediately after feeding and joined in parabiosis with a fifth stage larva, it moults into a diminutive 'adult'. The fifth stage provides the moulting hormone but clearly JH is absent. Wigglesworth also showed that JH is essential for the maintenance of larval characters. Parabiosis of a young larva onto a fifth instar larva, or implantation of corpora allata from young larvae, prevents metamorphosis and results, after moulting, in a perfect extra larval instar or a larval-adult intermediate.

Similar effects of JH have been demonstrated in many other species. In holometabolous insects, allatectomy (removal of corpora allata) of young larvae induces precocious pupation and, ultimately, small adults. Application of JH or corpus allatum implantation by contrast can produce large larvae by inducing extra larval stages; the adults produced finally can be 2-3 times their normal size. In general, the titre of JH is high during the larval stage and low or absent during the last larval instar (or during pupation) (Fig. 3.13). The levels rise again in the adult during reproductive development (Fig. 3.13; § 3.4.2).

In holometabolous insects adult tissues derive largely from the growth in the pupal stage of small islands of tissue (*imaginal discs*) which are present in the larval body, but quiescent, since embryogenesis. In hemimetabolous species the adult tissues form from the same cells (or their descendants) which formed the larval body. Evidently the larval cells carry a dual pattern: the visible larval and an invisible, adult pattern. In both Holometabola and Hemimetabola adult development requires a moult in the absence of JH; JH controls the degree and direction of differentiation at each moult, but how it does so is unclear. In adults, it stimulates vitellogenesis in the fat body (§ 3.4.2) by initiating the production of mRNA coded for specific vitellogenins, but it is not known whether JH in larvae exerts its morphogenetic properties by acting on nuclear genes or on factors in the cytoplasm.

The morphogenetic effectiveness of JH is dependent upon its time of release (or experimental application), and to be effective it must be present early in the instar. It acts prior to ecdysone i.e. before the cells divide (Fig. 3.5). Localized patches of larval cuticle often form, after the moult to adult, around sites of hormone application (see *Galleria* test p. 45); suggesting that JH acts directly on the epidermal cells. The target tissues are sensitive to JH for only a limited period, which differs between instars and between different parts of the body. Thus, in response to JH treatment, parts of the body may retain larval characters and other parts, which have lost their sensitivity to JH, develop adult characters. The complete retention of larval features is possible only if JH is present early in the instar; a complete switch to an adult form occurs when JH is absent during the sensitive periods of all tissues.

A moult may be thought of as a developmental gate which is split horizontally into several hinged sections, each unlocked by different titres of JH, the highest requiring high titres and the lowest requiring little or no JH. Thus as JH titre decreases, progressively lower sections open revealing more of the adult pattern. No gate sections can open if the master lock is closed; ecdysteroids open this master lock at each moult and in their absence no effects of JH are demonstrable. Such an analogy does not explain the mechanisms involved, but emphasizes that JH and ecdysone act in concert to control morphogenesis, though they act at different times and in different ways. Ecdysone can be thought of as playing a passive role, by timing events to indicate to the tissues whether or not they should proceed to develop. JH determines how far the cells shall progress along a particular morphogenetic programme, by switching on genes controlling larval pattern and suppressing genes for adult characters.

The interactions between JH and ecdysteroids are not understood fully. Allatectomy or application of excess exogenous JH can delay or inhibit moulting. The latter treatment, for example, can produce permanent larvae which will moult only when injected with ecdysone. Thus the lack of moulting in this instance is due to an endocrine deficiency, caused by excess of JH, and not to lack of responsiveness of the target tissues.

Transport of juvenile hormones

Juvenile hormone has a high solubility in aqueous media even though it is lipophilic. However, it is transported in the haemolymph attached to carrier proteins. Two kinds of JH-protein complexes form in the haemolymph. Albumins and lipoproteins form low affinity, low specificity, but high capacity interactions with JH; specific carrier proteins form complexes of high affinity, high specificity, but of low capacity. Similar transport systems exist in vertebrates for the transport of lipophilic hormones.

In *Manduca* the specific carrier protein is a single polypeptide containing no lipid and is 28 000 MWt, with a binding constant for JH-I of 3.3×10^{-6}M. During the fourth instar the titre of JH in the haemolymph is 3.3×10^{-9}M and the solubility of JH-I in aqueous media is 3.3×10^{-5}M; clearly there are sufficient sites on the binding protein for all the JH to be in the bound form. However, carrier proteins may have functions other than transport; possibly they are important in preventing the non-specific binding of the lipophilic JH to a variety of proteins and lipophilic surfaces. Carrier proteins may thus minimize the binding of JH by non-target cells so that the hormone is donated only to receptors with an affinity higher than that of the carrier proteins themselves.

Metabolism of juvenile hormones

Juvenile hormone is synthesized from acetate and propionates *via* mevalonate but the exact pathways are not known.

Two principal pathways exist for the degradation of JH (Fig. 3.14). Carboxyl esterase and epoxide hydrase occur in many tissues but the latter enzyme is absent from the haemolymph. The degradation products resulting from these enzymic actions are biologically inactive. The degradation of JH in the tissues is important but a critical factor is the presence and activity of esterases in the haemolymph, because their actions limit the amounts of JH reaching the target tissues. Two classes of esterase occur in haemolymph: general esterases cannot attack JH bound to specific carrier protein; JH-specific esterases attack both free JH and JH complexed with specific carrier protein. The role of these esterases in the regulation of JH titre is discussed below.

Titre of JH—Galleria test

Knowledge of variations in the titres of JH throughout development has come mostly from the use of bioassays (see Fig. 3.13). One widely used assay utilizes the wax moth, *Galleria*. In the test, young *Galleria* pupae are taken and a small wound made in their pronotal cuticle.

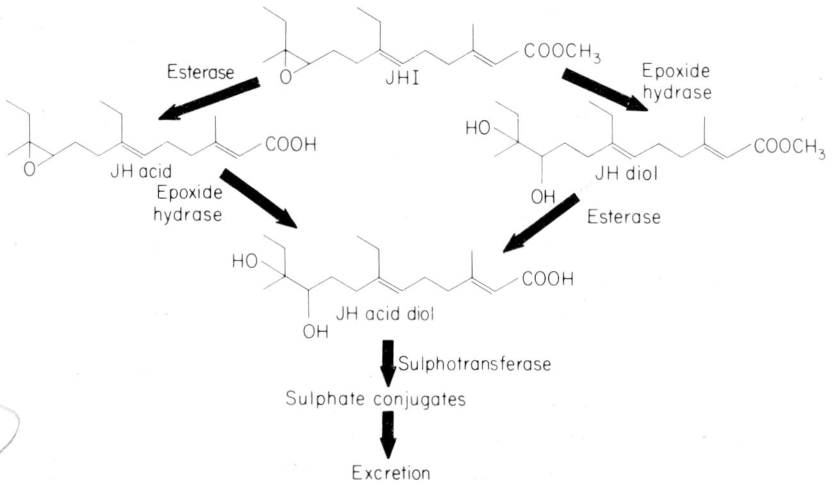

Fig. 3.14. Major catabolic pathways for juvenile hormone.

An aliquot of test extract containing JH is absorbed onto a 1 mm³ piece of paraffin wax and placed over the wound. The site of the wound is examined after the pupal-adult moult for the retention of pupal cuticle and the absence of adult scales. One 'Galleria unit' represents the activity of the test JH which results in 50% of the treated insects retaining pupal characters at the site of the treatment. Assay with synthetic JH shows this to be 2-5 pg (10^{-12} g) of JH-I or *c.* 25 pg of JH-III. In other assays which monitor the effects of JH upon ovarian growth, JH-III is three times more potent than JH-I. Such differences might be expected if JH-III is a gonadotropic hormone and JH-I a morphogenetic one.

The haemolymph titre of JH is determined by: the rates of synthesis and release of hormone, the activity of degradative enzymes, the amounts of carrier protein, hormone uptake into tissues and by excretion. The JH-specific esterases may play a crucial role in this but it is unlikely that a sufficiently fine control could be exerted throughout development by variations in enzyme levels. Other factors must also be involved. Specific carrier proteins (see above) afford protection against general esterases but not against specific esterases. Experiments in which the activity of the corpora allata are monitored *in vitro* show that glands vary their rate of synthesis and release of JH throughout adult development. It is likely that this is the major factor regulating JH-titre; the carrier proteins and degradative mechanisms merely attenuate the hormone signal.

Control of the corpora allata

The activity of the corpora allata could be regulated by neurosecretions, nervous control from the brain and/or suboesophageal ganglion, humoral factors or a combination of these. Unfortunately estimations of the rates of synthesis and release of JH are difficult to make *in vivo,* and indirect methods, such as histological studies, are of limited use in analyzing the dynamics of secretion. Direct measurements of synthesis, using radioactively labelled substrates and isolated glands have to be employed. Studies with isolated glands *in vitro* and results from implantation experiments show that isolated corpora allata function for considerable periods, once they have been 'switched on'. In some insects this switch is neurosecretion from the median cell group of the pars intercerebralis (Fig. 3.2); in others, secretions (or nerve impulses?) from the lateral neurosecretory cells have been implicated. In *Locusta* it has been suggested that antagonistic neurosecretions from the median cell group are involved, whereas in *Leucophaea* neurosecretions have been discounted and regulation is thought to be by nervous inhibition.

3.3.6 Hormones and polymorphism

Neurosecretory hormones and JH may both be involved in the control of polymorphism. JH controls morph determination in honey-bees and termites, and may be involved in the determination of the solitary phase in locusts. In aphids such as *Megoura,* virginoparae (parthenogenetic) forms appear in summer in response to long days (§ 7.5) but when the nights become longer than 10 h the embryos develop into sexually reproducing females (oviparae) with over-wintering eggs. The production of virginoparae is controlled by a specific group of neurosecretory cells in the brain whose product is transported axonally directly to the reproductive system. It is the brain and not the eyes which detect the changes in photoperiod. The other morphs in aphids are wingless (apterae) and winged (alatae); the switch between these is also hormonal but is not due to JH as was once thought. Apterae are produced as a response to lack of crowding and long days, alatae in response to short days and crowding. JH application produces wingless individuals but these are not typical apterae, the JH merely maintains larval (i.e. wingless) characters. It seems that the brain is involved again, possibly via specific groups of neurosecretory cells.

In termites and many other social insects, the environmental cues which regulate developmental events are pheromonal (§ 6.7.2) and 6.7.3). However, little is known of the detailed physiological mechanisms by which pheromones effect caste differentiation in social insects. For instance, it is not known whether the pheromones enter the responsive insect to exert a direct effect on target organs such as the ovary or the endocrine system, or whether they influence the endocrine system via the brain after stimulating specific receptors associated with the antennae or the mouthparts. Nevertheless, it is clear that the endocrine system, and particularly juvenile hormone from the corpora allata (§ 3.3.1 and 3.3.5), is intimately involved. In the honey-bee, for example, the undeveloped ovaries of workers correlate with their small, apparently inactive, corpora allata. In *Kalotermes,* removal of the royal pair initiates moulting in some pseudergates (Fig. 6.6) so quickly that it is assumed that some of the pheromones act directly on the brain to prevent activation of the prothoracic glands (§ 3.3.1). Undoubtedly, the activity of the corpora allata, which appears critical at all stages of termite development, is also influenced by pheromonal signals within the colony. Interestingly, work on *Kalotermes* suggested many years ago that the corpora allata produce more than one hormone, an interpretation which ran contrary to accepted dogma at that time. Briefly, this stemmed from the observation that adult corpora allata, but not those of larvae, could induce the development of soldiers from pseudergates—the gonadotropic activity of adult corpora allata was not therefore the same as the morphogenetic activity in larval corpora allata. Although this situation does not appear to have been clarified in *Kalotermes,* it is now accepted that the corpora allata of some insects do synthesize and release all three of the

known juvenile hormones and that these differ in their activities in different bioassays (§ 3.3.5).

3.4 ADULT GROWTH AND DEVELOPMENT

Somatic growth consists mainly of internal changes associated with the flight muscles, cuticle and fat body. Broadly, these changes are concerned with ensuring reproductive success. Thus, the flight muscles develop their full potential in terms of internal structure, stores of fuel and full complement of enzymes in preparation for migratory or mating flight (§ 7.3), and the fat body builds up stores of fat and/or carbohydrate to support such activity and the development of the accessory sex glands. Correspondingly, adult growth is often coincident with a period of feeding activity which may subsequently be repeated for each cycle of reproductive activity. Almost nothing is known concerning the control of adult growth and, as with the juvenile stages, there is no evidence for the existence of a general growth hormone. On the other hand the processes of sexual

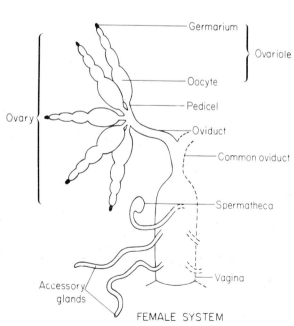

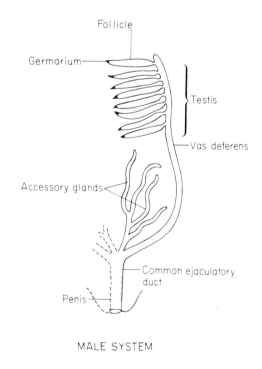

Fig. 3.15. Diagram of male and female reproductive systems in a generalized insect. Only half of the system is shown for each sex.

maturare are under endocrine control in most insects. In addition, in many insects *pheromones* (chemicals produced by one individual which affect the physiology or behaviour of another of the same species § 6.6) play a large part in the development of sexual maturity, and in bringing the sexes together for mating. Perhaps this is best exemplified in locusts, where reproductive synchrony is established in the population by pheromones which either accelerate the slow developers or slow down the precocious individuals. The production of such pheromones is often under hormonal control; in adult male *Schistocerca,* the production in the epidermis of a pheromone, which stimulates maturation in other males and elicits behavioural and physiological responses in mature females, is under the control of secretions from the corpora allata.

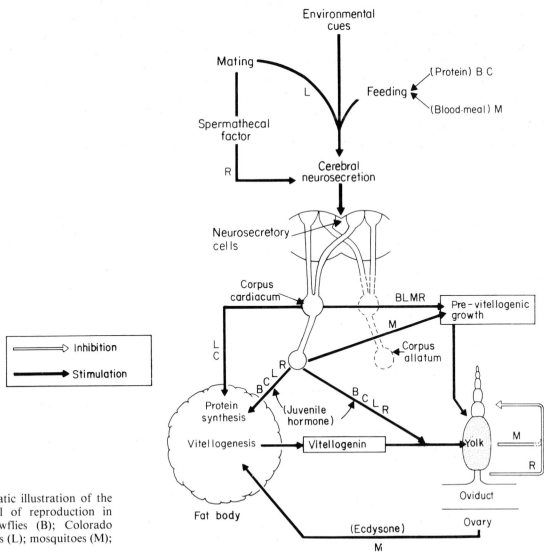

Fig. 3.16. Schematic illustration of the endocrine control of reproduction in five insects: blowflies (B); Colorado beetles (C); locusts (L); mosquitoes (M); *Rhodnius* (R).

3.4.1   Reproduction

The production of gametes

The gonads are paired abdominal structures (although the testes of some species are fused into a single medial body) consisting of a variable number of ovarioles (in ovaries) or follicles (in testes) each having a distal germarium (Fig. 3.15). Mature eggs or sperm pass down paired oviducts or vasa deferentia to meet with secretions from accessory glands in a common vagina or ejaculatory duct (Fig. 3.15).

The ovaries of more primitive insects such as dragonflies and locusts, are panoistic: each daughter cell of the oogonia develops into an oocyte surrounded by follicle cells which are involved in the pre-vitellogenic stages of growth and later in yolk deposition (§ 3.4.2), and which eventually secrete the shell or chorion. In most holometabolous insects, e.g. Diptera, the ovaries are meroistic, and only one of the daughter cells from each oogonium develops into an oocyte—the remaining ones form trophic 'nurse' cells closely associated with the oocyte. In bugs and in some beetles, the nurse cells remain in the germarium and retain contact with the oocyte developing in the ovariole by a long nutritive cord. However, even in meroistic ovaries, the nurse cells degenerate at the beginning of yolk deposition and the follicle cells then control the development of the oocytes and form the chorion. Nutritive cells are similarly involved during spermatogenesis in the testis.

Mating

In most insects the transfer of sperm from the male to the female involves either direct deposition of sperm into a special storage reservoir in the female, the spermatheca (Fig. 3.15) or the placing of a package of sperm, the *spermatophore,* inside the genital opening of the female. In some insects secretions of the male, transferred to the female at mating, affect female reproductive activity (Fig. 3.16) often preventing further mating and reducing female responsiveness to subsequent advances by other males. Female secretions liberate the sperm from the spermatophore and contractions of the female tract transfer sperm to the spermatheca.

The synthesis of materials for spermatophore production occurs in the male accessory glands which are subject to control from the adult corpora allata. While spermatogenesis and the early stages of oogenesis proceed independently of the adult endocrine system, the later stages of oocyte development (see below) and, in some species, sexual behaviour and/or the production of pheromones are controlled by hormones (§ 6.4).

3.4.2   Endocrine control of sexual development

With one known exception, the glow-worm beetle, *Lampyris,* the morphological differences between the sexes are genetically determined and secondary sexual characters are therefore largely unaffected by hormones. Some aspects of behaviour and body pigmentation associated with reproduction are, however, controlled by the endocrine system; as indeed is the production of mature eggs in most insects. This is important because most insects must ensure that reproductive effort is initiated only when conditions are suitable for success. By contrast, in those species in which adult life is short and reproduction commences immediately the adult emerges, the adult endocrine system does not influence egg development.

Reproductive physiology in female insects has been investigated extensively in only a few species. No simple pattern of control emerges; each species differs in detail and Fig. 3.16 shows some of the known variations between species. The cerebral neurosecretory cells are necessary for oocyte development, either directly (at the pre-vitellogenic stage) or, in some species, indirectly via a general stimulatory effect on protein synthesis in the fat body. In many insects the cerebral neurosecretory cells initiate reproductive development in response to appropriate environmental information; this initiation may involve activating the corpora allata. The synthesis of yolk precursors (*vitellogenins*) occurs in the fat body and in most insects is stimulated by a juvenile hormone from the corpora allata (§ 3.3.5). In mosquitoes, however, ecdysone from the ovaries stimulates vitellogenesis (Fig. 3.16). The occurrence of ecdysone in adult insects is surprising since the prothoracic glands (p. 34) degenerate in adult pterygote insects. However, species other than the mosquito are known to synthesize ecdysone in the adult ovary, though only in the mosquito is it known to be released into the haemolymph.

Juvenile hormone may also stimulate yolk deposition in developing oocytes (Fig. 3.16) by inducing the formation of spaces between the follicle cells to allow vitellogenins access to the surface of the oocyte. In some insects inhibitory feedback from fully developed oocytes, or from the pedicel (Fig. 3.16), inhibits the development of pre-vitellogenic oocytes; this may be a direct effect via a 'local hormone' or it may involve the cerebral neurosecretory cells. There is considerable uncertainty concerning the interactions between the endocrine centres involved in the control of ovarian function, particularly as to the roles of the neurosecretory cells and the corpora allata. When a clearer picture emerges it is certain that the control system will be found to be complex.

3.4.3   Ageing in adults

After the attainment of sexual maturity, insects often show degenerative changes in reproductive and flight performance which can be called ageing. Such ageing phenomena have received considerable attention in the Diptera especially in relation to the deterioration of flight performance. Characteristically, the duration of sustained flight decreases with age and this has been correlated with a number of ultrastructural and bio-chemical changes in the flight muscles, but other tissues, such as the nervous system and the fat body may also be involved. The orderly and sequential changes in the ageing phenomena which correlate with biochemical changes suggest that ageing is not simply due to random error but is programmed. In locusts, ageing may be influenced by the activity of the corpora allata; when these glands are removed the locusts live longer and show a number of features, including improved flight performance, which suggest that ageing has been slowed considerably. The situation is complex, however, since removal of the ovaries from locusts results in premature ageing (though this can be reversed if the corpora allata are removed also). Experiments with synthetic juvenile hormone mimics (§3.6) suggest that it is the juvenile hormone (or its absence) which is responsible for these effects but the mechanism by which ageing is influenced is unknown.

3.5   DIAPAUSE—HORMONAL CONTROL

Many insects enter periods of developmental arrest, or diapause, to circumvent unfavourable environmental conditions (§7.5). For some species, this is an obligatory event in their life history; for others, it intervenes during development only under certain conditions and is then said to be facultative. The most common form of diapause is that of overwintering by pupae, but repro-ductive diapause can occur in adults, and overwintering may occur both in larvae and in eggs. Whether diapause is obligatory or facultative, the insects respond to environmental cues which are used to 'predict' the future onset of unfavourable conditions. These cues include temperature (§ 7.2), lack of moisture, population density, and especially photoperiod (§ 7.5).

Larval and pupal diapause are caused by inactivity of the cerebral neurosecretory cells which cease to release brain hormone; the consequent lack of moulting hormone results in failure to moult. Neurosecretory cells can respond directly to light, being inactivated by short photoperiods and activated by long photoperiods (though other mechanisms of photoperiodic induction also occur—§ 7.5). The cerebral neurosecretory cells of many overwintering pupae need a considerable period of cold exposure before they can be reactivated. Adult reproductive diapause may be caused by inactivity of the corpora allata, since the diapause state often resembles that caused by their removal. For example, in the Colorado beetle, diapause is initiated rapidly in short days, but reproductive development can be restored temporarily by the implantation of active corpora allata or the application of JH-I. Implantation of brains from active beetles will, however, cause a complete break (termination) of diapause. It seems that in these beetles arrest of reproductive development is brought about by a rapid inhibition of the corpora allata in response to short day conditions, but the diapause state is maintained by subsequent inactivity of the cerebral neurosecretory cells. One of the effects of JH-I applica-tion to diapausing beetles is an immediate release of stored cerebral neurosecretion. Under long day conditions, this causes complete diapause break. In short days, however, this treatment merely produces a temporary return to reproductive development, because the neurosecretory cells in the brain are inactive.

Embryonic or egg diapause in the silkmoth, *Bombyx,* is not caused by the *absence* of developmental hormones but by the *presence* of a specific diapause hormone in the female which affects the developing oocytes. *Bombyx* is bivoltine (§ 7.5) and only eggs laid in the winter enter diapause. Long days and high temperatures in the summer affect the developing eggs so that the pupae which develop from them release diapause hormone. This comes from a pair of neurosecretory cells in the sub-oesophageal ganglion (Fig. 3.2). It affects the deposition of glycogen and yolk in the developing oocytes (egg development commences in the pupae of silkmoths) so that when the eggs are laid they will enter diapause and overwinter. The short days and low temperature during winter act on these eggs to prevent any subsequent release of diapause hormone in the pupae which develop ultimately from winter (diapause) eggs; eggs laid in the summer are non-diapause eggs. The pupal brain controls the release of diapause hormone from the sub-oesophageal ganglion, but the mechanism by which environmental information from the embryo and (to a lesser extent) the early larval stages is stored, and eventually influences the activity of the pupal brain, is unknown. This problem of information storage is not unique to *Bombyx;* in many insects environmental changes which initiate diapause, may occur a considerable time before the actual arrest of development.

3.6   INSECT GROWTH REGULATORS

'Insect growth regulators' are compounds which can be used as insecticides, to disrupt the normal development of insects. In reality they are no different in intent from conventional insecticides: they are designed to kill or debilitate insects. The term is something of a misnomer in that the compounds do not necessarily disrupt growth as such but interfere with programmes of development and differentiation.

The initial concept behind regulators of the hormone-mimic kind was to apply a compound to larval insects to prevent metamorphosis, i.e. to act as JH-mimics. It is obvious that such compounds will be effective against only the last larval stage and compounds with this limited action have little potential. Several other compounds have been developed which not only disrupt meta-

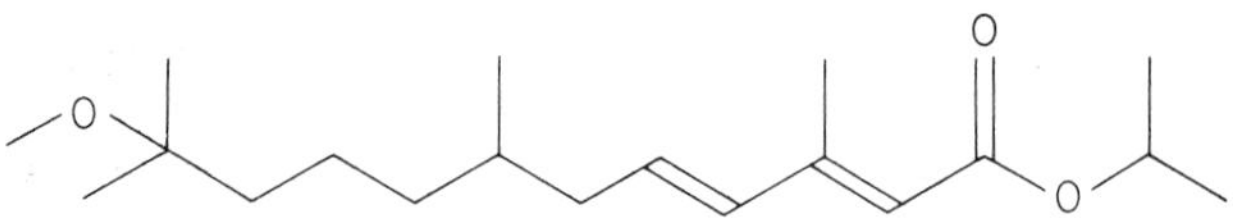

ALTOSID, ZR-515 (Zoecon Corporation)

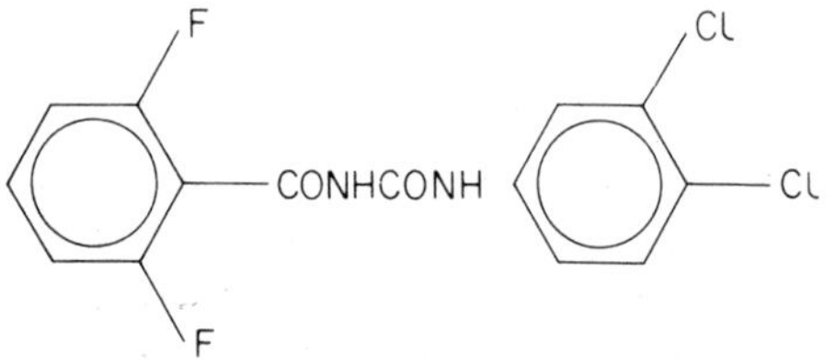

DIMILIN, PH-60-40 (Phillips Duphar)

Fig. 3.17. Altosid is the first morphogenic agent to be recognized formally by the United States Environmental Protection Agency. It is being employed against mosquitoes. Other possible uses include its incorporation in cattle feed to control fly larvae in cattle dung. Compare the structure of Altosid with JH (Fig. 3.11). Dimilin is one of a class of benzoyl phenyl ureas which interfere with cuticle deposition. The compound is active when ingested, and if applied to larvae causes a disruption in moulting.

morphosis but possess a distinct additional advantage in that they interfere with the hormonal control of moulting and thus are effective at every instar. Other compounds may interfere with chitin deposition and in consequence produce deformed cuticles and non-viable insects (Fig. 3.17). It is difficult to generalize about growth regulators because a wide variety of compounds is involved and the structures of many have not been released by commercial developers. Two major categories exist, those which exhibit high specificity and could be used selectively against pests without harming useful insects and those with a broad spectrum activity.

Further reading

Highnam K. C. & Hill, L. (1977) *The Comparative Endo-crinology of the Invertebrates.* (Chap. 6, 7, & 8). Edward Arnold.

Lawrence P. A. (Ed.) (1976) *Insect Development. Symp. R. ent. Soc., Lond.,* **8** Blackwell Scientific Publications.

Wigglesworth V. B. (1959) *The Control of Growth & Form.* Cornell University Press.

Chapter 4
Nervous and Sensory
Systems

A substantial part of the capacity of an insect to regulate its relationships with its internal and external environments depends on its electrically excitable cells. Such cells occur in the sense organs, the nervous system and the muscles. They detect stimuli, process information, and co-ordinate responses by their mutual electrical interactions. Sensory cells utilize as a trigger the energy, usually meagre, to which the environment characteristically subjects them—the energy of the gravitational field, the vibrational energy of particles conveying sound, the energy of electromagnetic radiation, the potential energy of chemicals, etc. In receptor neurones, the general irritability of protoplasm is enhanced for a particular stimulus modality and there may be accessory structures present which make the incident energy more effective. Whatever the stimulus modality, the receptor cell acts as a transducer and biological amplifier, transposing stimulus energy into electrical energy, the common currency of the neuromuscular and sensory systems.

4.1 THE NERVE CELLS

Most insect neurones are monopolar, that is, a single long filamentous axon arises from the cell body and gives off shorter branches (Fig. 4.1, d,c). These branches have terminal arborizations at which contact is made with other neurones by way of synapses (§ 4.6). Insect receptor cells, however, are usually bipolar, having a cell body in, or immediately under the epidermis and sending a short, single dendrite to a sense organ in the cuticle, and a long axon to the central nervous system (Fig. 4.1,a). Soft-skinned larvae have multipolar receptor cells whose numerous, finely branching dendrites anastomose to form a sub-epidermal plexus Fig. 4.1,b).

4.2 THE ORGANIZATION OF THE NERVOUS SYSTEM

Bundles of axons run together in the body and constitute the 'nerves', but the cell bodies of most neurones, as well as many of their projections, are contained entirely within the nerve ganglia. These segmentally arranged ganglia are united by paired longitudinal connectives and constitute the central nervous system (CNS). The ganglia consist of the fused left and right lateral ganglia, reflecting the insect's primitive bilateral symmetry. Evolution has led to centralization along the longitudinal axis and has resulted in a reduction of segmental autonomy. The brain (Fig. 4.2), consisting of the fused ganglia of three pre-oral segments, is the principal association centre of the nervous system, and is the seat of initiation and control of persistent behavioural patterns. Additionally, it modifies the more immediate responses arising in other parts of the nervous system and in the brain itself (§6.1). The ganglia of the first three post-oral segments have fused to form the sub-oesophageal ganglion. In the thorax and abdomen, the segmental ganglia may be identified separately along the double ventral nerve cord, but in the higher insects, some fusion, especially of abdominal ganglia, may occur.

A fairly constant structural organization is found within the ganglia. The neuronal cell bodies (*perikarya*) are located at the periphery, while the central region is occupied by a complex network of nerve cell processes called the *neuropile*. Each neurone is almost completely ensheathed by one or more *glial cells,* but at synapses (§4.6) the glial sheath is absent. Synapses always occur between nerve processes, rather than with cell bodies as occurs in vertebrates. Many of the glial cells have processes extending inwards from the periphery of the

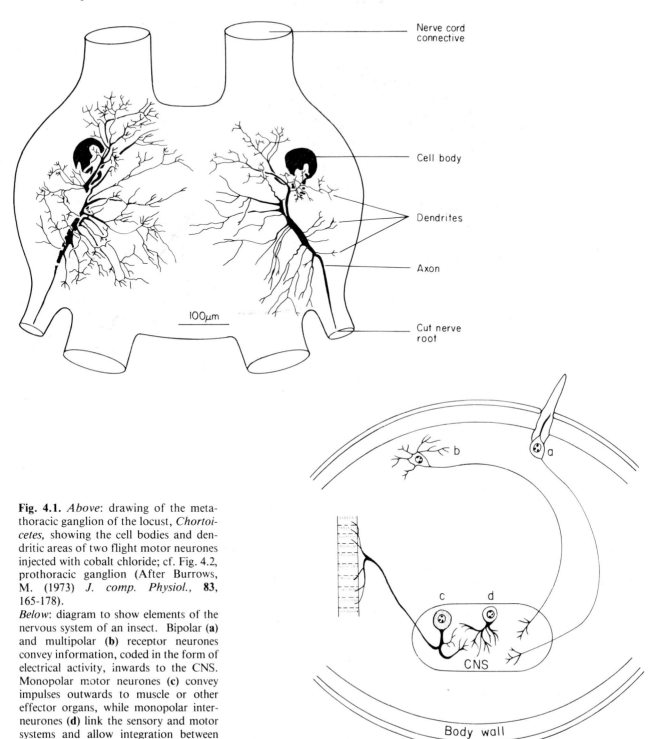

Fig. 4.1. *Above*: drawing of the metathoracic ganglion of the locust, *Chortoicetes,* showing the cell bodies and dendritic areas of two flight motor neurones injected with cobalt chloride; cf. Fig. 4.2, prothoracic ganglion (After Burrows, M. (1973) *J. comp. Physiol.,* **83**, 165-178).

Below: diagram to show elements of the nervous system of an insect. Bipolar (**a**) and multipolar (**b**) receptor neurones convey information, coded in the form of electrical activity, inwards to the CNS. Monopolar motor neurones (**c**) convey impulses outwards to muscle or other effector organs, while monopolar interneurones (**d**) link the sensory and motor systems and allow integration between them.

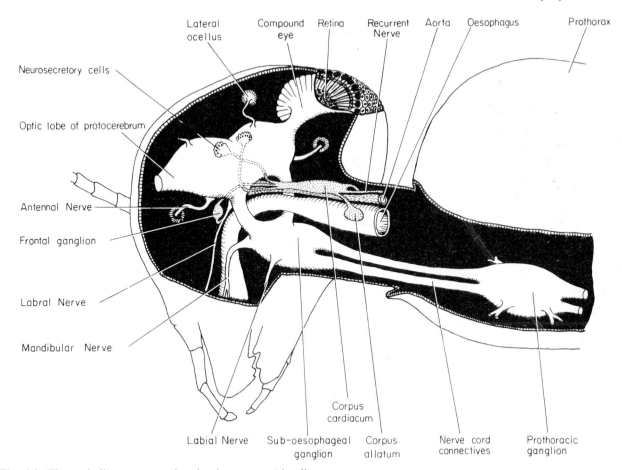

Lateral ocellus — Compound eye — Retina — Recurrent Nerve — Aorta — Oesophagus — Prothorax

Neurosecretory cells

Optic lobe of protocerebrum

Antennal Nerve

Frontal ganglion

Labral Nerve

Mandibular Nerve

Labial Nerve — Sub-oesophageal ganglion — Corpus cardiacum — Corpus allatum — Nerve cord connectives — Prothoracic ganglion

Fig. 4.2. The cephalic nervous and endocrine system (simplified) of a typical insect. The size of the ganglia is slightly exaggerated, and many minor nerves are omitted. (see also Fig. 3.2, p. 34)

ganglion, and one of their functions is to convey nutrients to the neurones whose cell bodies, lying within the ganglia, are relatively distant from the haemolymph. The outer layer of glial cells that lines the surface of the ganglia and nerve cord forms the *perineurium*; its cells are rich in glycogen granules and fat globules. In addition to its role of storage and transfer of nutrients and metabolites, the perineurium separates the nerve cells from the haemolymph. The insulation afforded by this 'blood-brain barrier' is important for the proper functioning of the nerve cells (§4.4).

Further protection of the CNS is provided by the *neural lamella,* a non-cellular sheath external to the perineurium consisting of collagen-like fibres embedded in a mucopolysaccharide and mucoprotein matrix. The smaller, peripheral nerves are also sheathed and protected, though generally to a lesser extent.

Another series of small ganglia and their associated nerves constitute the sympathetic or *visceral nervous system* which innervates the alimentary canal. It consists of the stomatogastric system supplying the anterior part of the gut and some neighbouring structures and, posteriorly, the ventral sympathetic system including nerves to the hind-gut and the reproductive organs. Various parts of the endocrine system are closely associated with the nervous system (§3.3.1).

4.3   NEURONAL FUNCTIONING

Because of the small diameter of most axons, they are difficult to penetrate with micro-capillary electrodes. Thus most of our knowledge of axonal functioning is derived from studies on giant axons which occur in the CNS of some animals. The pioneering work in this field was carried out on squid giant axons by Hodgkin and Huxley and their colleagues (see Hodgkin, A. L. (1958), *Proc. R. Soc. B.* **148**, 1-37). Work on the giant axons of the cockroach, *Periplaneta americana,* suggests that the mechanisms involved are essentially the same as those elucidated for the squid.

4.3.1   The properties of neurones and the action potential

The ability of neurones to function in their characteristic manner is due mainly to the properties of their cell membranes. These are semi-permeable and effectively separate two ion-containing compartments: the cell contents and the external medium. The system so formed, supplemented by an active ion pump in the axon membrane, is subject to the laws of ionic diffusion and osmosis, and particularly to the Donnan equilibrium. A fuller account of these phenomena will be found in Aidley (1971). The membrane is much more permeable to K^+ than Na^+ and this, together with the unequal concentrations of Na^+, K^+ and Cl^- inside and outside the cell, establishes a state of polarization across the membrane so that it is about 70 mV more positive on the outside than on the inside. This is known as the *resting potential,* and an increase in polarization is called a *hyperpolarization,* whilst a decrease is called a *depolarization.* The charged membrane acts as an energy store which is utilized when the cell responds to stimulation.

When a depolarizing current pulse is applied through electrodes in contact with an axon, the response in the axons depends on the magnitude of the current pulse (Fig. 4.3). In the graded, *passive response* (Fig. 4.3a) all the energy derives from the applied pulse. However, the *local potential* (Fig. 4.3b), which is also graded and proportional to the applied pulse, results from a change of membrane permeability and uses some of the energy of polarization stored in the neurone, i.e. it is an 'active' response. Both passive and local potentials decay exponentially from their point of initiation, but when the depolarization reaches a threshold level, a dramatic change in membrane permeability occurs, resulting in the *action potential* or *spike* (Fig. 4.3c). Na^+ ions flow inwards through the membrane during the rapid depolarization or rising phase, and K^+ ions flow outwards during the repolarization, or falling phase. The potential change experienced during the spike causes local currents to flow through the adjacent membrane, depolarizing it above the threshold level so that the spike is propagated away from its point of initiation. When a spike has occurred, the membrane is incapable of a similar response for a short time afterwards. This is the *refractory period.*

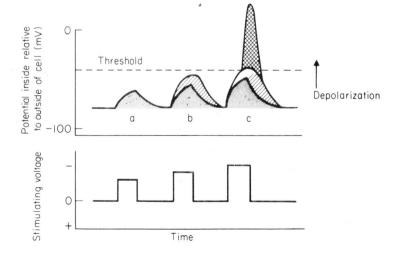

Fig. 4.3. The axon membrane response (upper diagram) to application of square pulses of current (lower diagram). ▦ The graded passive response (at a, b, c). ▨ The graded local potential. ▧ The action potential, which is not graded and is initiated when the membrane potential reaches the threshold level (dashed line) (After Florey E. (1966) *An Introduction to General and Comparative Animal Physiology,* W. B. Saunders, Philadelphia).

4.3.2 Neuronal phenomena

In each neurone, one or more regions, located on dendrites (Fig. 4.1), differs from the axon in membrane properties. It is in these *receptor regions* that electrical activity is initiated. In receptor neurones, these regions respond to external stimuli, but in interneurones and motor neurones the source of initiation is synaptic transmission (§ 4.6). In all cases, the stimulus energy is transduced and amplified to form the *receptor potential,* which spreads to the spike-generating region of the neurone which is usually situated where the axon joins the cell body. Here it initiates a local potential and, if the threshold is reached, one or more spikes will be produced (Fig. 4.4). The strength of the stimulus is represented first in analogue form, as a graded receptor potential, and is then encoded in digital form as action potentials by the spike-initiating region of the neurone.

The process of *accommodation* (Fig. 4.4) allows not only the magnitude of the stimulus but also its duration and rate of change to be represented by the spike code. In accommodation, the receptor membrane reacts against the stimulus so that the receptor potential tends to return to the resting level. If the onset of a stimulus is gradual, accommodation may result in a receptor potential too small to initiate spikes, and the stimulus goes 'unnoticed'. Conversely a stimulus whose intensity changes rapidly is much more likely to be detected. A stimulus of constant amplitude and long duration, if initially above threshold level, will result in a train of spikes whose frequency declines due to accommodation (Fig. 4.4). This effect is known as *adaptation.*

In general, the rate of accommodation of a neurone is appropriate for the type of stimulus it has to monitor. In some receptor cells, accommodation is rapid and the cell responds with a brief burst of action potentials. This is called a *phasic response,* and *phasic receptors* occur in situations where it is important for the insect to receive reports on changes of stimulation which may follow each other rapidly. Conversely, if accommodation occurs slowly, a receptor will continue to respond to a steady stimulus for a much longer time. This is called a *tonic response,* and *tonic receptors* monitor persistent steady stimuli. In practice, many receptors are phasico-tonic, that is, they respond to the onset of a stimulus with a high rate of firing, which then declines to a lower steady level.

Some receptor neurones, and many neurones of the CNS, produce a constant stream of action potentials even in apparently unstimulated conditions. This is due to a persistent local potential above the threshold level. Such neurones may be affected by stimuli so that their free-running activity is increased or decreased. Environmental stimuli which affect the generator membrane

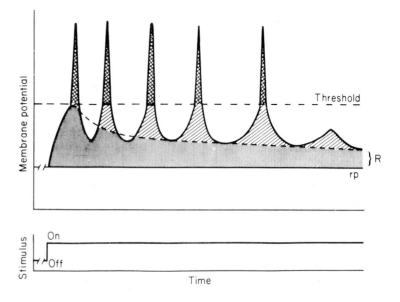

Fig. 4.4. The effect of accommodation on the rate of generation of action potentials. The stimulus of constant amplitude (lower diagram) results in a receptor potential (R) which declines towards the resting potential (rp), due to accommodation. Superimposed on the receptor potential are other active local potentials initiated by it. They develop after the refractory period following each spike and take progressively longer to reach the threshold level as the receptor potential declines. The decline in firing rate, and sometimes ultimate cessation of firing, is called adaptation. ▨ Local potentials ⊠ action potentials. (After Florey see Fig. 3.3.).

to cause depolarization and increased firing rate are called *excitatory stimuli.* Those causing hyperpolarization and decreased firing are called *inhibitory stimuli.*

4.4 THE BLOOD-BRAIN BARRIER

Neuronal functioning in insects, as in other animals, is profoundly affected by the ionic composition of the fluid bathing the cells, and requires relatively high concentrations of Na$^+$ in the extra-axonal fluid. The extent to which the ionic composition of the haemolymph, which bathes the nervous system, varies from species to species, and from time to time in the same species is therefore surprising. Particularly remarkable are those phytophagous insects with high levels of potassium and low levels of sodium in their haemolymph. If the perineurium (p. 55) is removed to expose the neurones to the haemolymph, their functioning is greatly impaired or totally prevented.

This argues for the presence of a barrier between the haemolymph and the fluid film bathing the neurones. Ultrastructural studies, using electron-opaque tracer molecules of appropriate dimensions, indicate that water-soluble ions easily penetrate intercellularly through the fatty sheath and neural lamella but are blocked at the perineurium by tight junctions between cells.

This *blood-brain barrier* is not simply a passive diffusion barrier, but involves active transport of ions between the fluid around the axons and the haemolymph (see §2.1). When the cockroach nervous system is bathed in sodium-deficient saline there is a gradual decline in occurrence of action potentials, but on return to normal saline, the system recovers rapidly. This recovery is evidently due to an active process since it is slowed down by inhibitors of sodium transport. This evidence, and measurements of potassium flux, suggest that the blood-brain barrier involves a linked Na$^+$/K$^+$ pump which is probably located on the membranes adjacent to the extra-axonal space, involving perineurial and glial cells.

4.5 RECEPTOR FUNCTIONING

In mechanoreceptor and chemoreceptor neurones (Fig. 4.5), the receptor regions (§4.3.1) of the cell membranes are situated at the tips of the dendrites. The membrane itself at this region shows no distinguishing features, even at the magnification of the electron microscope. Within the cytoplasm of the dendrite a variable number of microtubules lie parallel to the long axis of the dendrite. At the extreme end of mechanoreceptor dendrites the microtubules are more numerous and are interlinked to form a tubular body. No such structure is found in chemoreceptors. In light-sensitive neurones the dendrite is absent and the receptor region is believed to be an area of cell body membrane which consists of numerous microvilli. This region is called a *rhabdomere.* Receptor neurones may occur singly or in groups. They are usually surrounded by sheathing cells, and associated with an area of cuticle which is modified to gather stimuli of the appropriate modality and increase the effectiveness with which they impinge on the receptor region. Such composite structures are called *sensilla*—singular, *sensillum* (Fig. 4.5).

4.5.1 The sensilla

Mechanoreceptor neurones occur most commonly in *trichoid sensilla* (Fig. 4.5A), which consist of socketed hairs arranged so that when the hair is bent in its socket, the dendritic ending located at the hair base is deformed (§4.5.2). In *campaniform sensilla* (Fig. 4.5B), which lack a hair, stimulation of the dendrite results from deformation of the dome by stresses in the cuticle. Stretch receptors occur within the body, often not associated with cuticle. *Chemoreceptors* may also take the form of trichoid sensilla, but with the dendrites from several neurones exposed to the environment by pores in the hair wall (one apical pore in 'taste' or contact chemoreceptors (Fig. 4.5C) or hundreds of minute pores in olfactory receptors). In some chemoreceptors the hair is reduced or replaced by a porous plate through which chemicals can reach the dendritic endings. A number of sensilla, structurally similar to chemoreceptors, have been implicated in the sensitivity shown by many insects to temperature and to humidity.

A dermal light sense occurs in many insects, but associated sense organs have never been found. Dorsal and lateral *ocelli* contain light-sensitive neurones surrounded by pigment cells and associated with light-gathering lenses. The *compound eyes* have the same three elements but are more complex in structure (Fig.

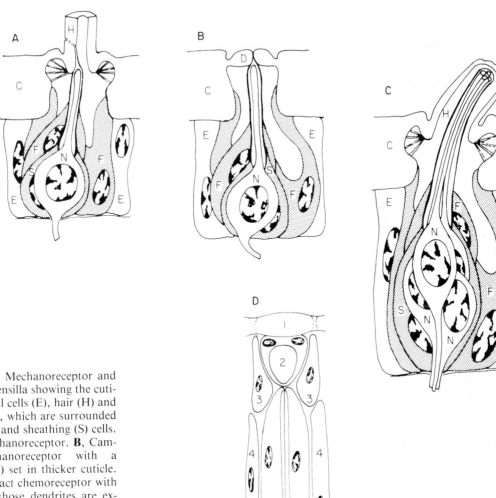

Fig. 4.5. **(A)-(C)** Mechanoreceptor and chemoreceptor sensilla showing the cuticle (C), epidermal cells (E), hair (H) and the neurones (N), which are surrounded by formative (F) and sheathing (S) cells. **A**, Trichoid mechanoreceptor. **B**, Campaniform mechanoreceptor with a slender dome (D) set in thicker cuticle. **C**, Trichoid contact chemoreceptor with four neurones whose dendrites are exposed at the single pore at the hair tip. (After Blaney, W. M. & Chapman, R. F. (1969) *J. Zool., Lond.,* **157**, 509-535). **D**, A single ommatidium of a compound eye showing: 1, the cuticular lens; 2, the crystalline cone; 3, primary pigment cells; 4, secondary pigment cells; 5, retinula cells, the sensory neurones with central microvillar borders (the rhabdomeres, 6), believed to be the location of visual pigment.

4.5D). There may be hundreds, even thousands, of *ommatidia* (each equivalent to a single sensillum) grouped together in each compound eye. The main lens of the ommatidium is the crystalline cone, which forms a small erect image of its field of view. However, there are only 7-8 retinula cells (the sensory cells) in each ommatidium, too few to resolve this image. Instead, each ommatidium registers the average light intensity of that part of the visual field which it faces, the screening pigment preventing spread of light between ommatidia,

Fig. 4.6. Diagrams to show the paths of light rays through **A**, apposition and **B**, superposition compound eyes. L-L, the lens system of individual ommatidia separated by pigment (P); R-R, the rhabdom regions of the ommatidia. In the apposition eye, the pigment sleeves absorb light which has entered the ommatidia obliquely so that each ommatidium responds only to the light from the small area of the visual field which it faces. In the superposition eye, each rhabdom may receive light entering a number of ommatidia, so that this type of eye is more sensitive in low light conditions. The images formed by the lens systems of individual ommatidia enlarge and overlap to form a somewhat blurred 'superposition' image at the level of the rhabdoms.

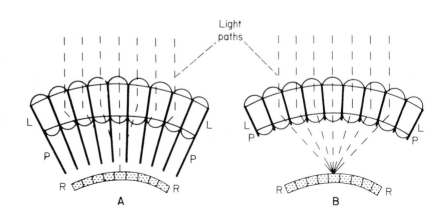

and the whole eye forms a mosaic image by the *apposition* of adjacent spots of light (Fig. 4.6A). This type of eye is found in diurnal insects. In many nocturnal insects, the screening pigment can move within the cells. In bright light, the pigment extends between the ommatidia as in the apposition eye, but in dim light the pigment withdraws so that the groups of retinula cells are no longer screened from each other, and the images spread and superimpose on each other deeper in the eye (Fig. 4.6B). In such *superposition* eyes, the image is less sharply defined than in the apposition eye but less of the light is absorbed by the screening pigment, so that the ommatidium is more sensitive at low light intensities.

As well as having a wide range of sensitivity, compound eyes often respond to polarized light and to colour, and their image-forming apparatus allows form discrimination and efficient detection of movement.

4.5.2 Transduction

When a receptor neurone is affected by a stimulus, the cell responds electrically, regardless of the modality of the original stimulus. The process by which the stimulus energy affects the receptor membrane, causing a change in the permeability of the membrane to some ions, and the consequent development of a receptor potential, is called transduction. As the nature of the stimulus energy varies with different stimulus modalities, so the process of transduction to electrical energy varies, but in no case is it fully understood.

The process could simply be a direct mechanical one, mechanical stress applied to the receptor membrane altering ion pores and consequently membrane permeability. In many mechanoreceptors, transduction appears to be associated with compression of the bundle of microtubules in the tip of the dendrite. In others, with a rather different neurotubular cytoskeleton in the dendrite tip, bending the hair stretches the membrane over the cytoskeleton. In either case, the stimulus may excite, either by altering membrane capacitance or by altering ionic conductance.

The mechanisms of conductance change are no better understood in chemoreceptors. It is usually assumed that a change of conductance of the dendrite membrane results from the interaction of an *acceptor protein,* located in the receptor membrane, with a stimulus molecule. The acceptor protein may react with the stimulus and undergo a structural change which could affect the ion pores and membrane permeability. In olfactory sensilla on the antennae of *Locusta,* which are sensitive to hexanoic acids, the molecular configuration of the stimulating molecule is critically important in determining stimulating power. There is some evidence to suggest enzyme involvement in chemoreception, based on the affinity between acceptor (enzyme) and stimulus (substrate). For example, sugar reception in blowfly taste sensilla may involve a reaction between the sugar and an *α*-glucosidase present in the receptor membrane. This enzyme is found in the tips of the sensilla and the concentration of sugar needed to reach the threshold for a receptor response (determined electrophysiologically) is compatible with the affinity of the isolated enzyme for its substrate (determined biochemically).

Knowledge of transduction in visual receptors is also incomplete. The photopigment is always a retinal-protein complex. Most insects are probably capable of colour vision, and pigments which absorb maximally at different wavelengths of light occur in different receptor cells. An electrogenic ion pump (§ 2.1) may contribute to the maintenance of the resting potential in receptor cells, and it has been suggested that modulation of such a pump by light could create the receptor potential. However, most evidence supports the hypothesis that illumination results in an increase in conductance of the photoreceptor membrane and that an influx of Na^+ produces the receptor potential. How this mechanism is linked to light absorbance by the photopigment is not known.

4.5.3 Coding of information

Within each stimulus modality there are many variations in stimulus quality (different colours in photoreception, different tastes or smells in chemoreception), and other parameters of each quality may also vary (e.g. intensity or rate of change). In most sensory systems, the magnitude of the receptor potential is proportional to the log of the stimulus intensity. This enables a receptor to respond to a wide range of stimulus intensities. Some *specialist* receptor cells, however, are only responsive to small changes in one parameter of a narrowly defined quality of a single modality of stimulus, while other, *generalist* receptors have a wide range of responsiveness.

The representation of various aspects of a stimulus in terms of a spike frequency code has been described in §4.3.2, and applies to most receptor cells. The mechanisms of coding in visual receptors is different, however. The receptor potential developed in retinula cells is propagated by electrotonic spread, without spike

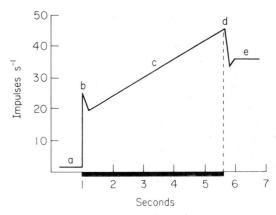

Fig. 4.7. The output from a stretch receptor in the dorsal longitudinal muscle of the larva of *Antheraea* before, during and after steady stretching. Thick bar on ordinate shows period of stretching. Response shows: (a) tonic level of firing; (b) response due to acceleration of stretching; (c) increasing tonic level superimposed on phasic response to constant velocity stretching; (d) response due to deceleration; (e) new tonic level (After Weevers, R. deG. (1966) *J. exp. Biol.,* **44**, 177-194).

initiation, to influence the second-order neurones in the optic lobe of the brain.

In mechanoreceptors and chemoreceptors the output is a train of spikes, the flow of which varies with the characteristics of the receptor. Thus, a phasic mechanoreceptor may signal movement, a tonic mechanoreceptor may signal position, a muscle stretch receptor may signal both (Fig. 4.7) and all three can register different intensity of stimulus. Some chemoreceptor neurones are highly specific in their sensitivity to one particular compound or group of closely related compounds. They include the specialist olfactory neurones in the antennae of some male moths that respond almost exclusively to the pheromone emitted by the female of the same species (§6.6), and possibly the 'taste' receptors of some phytophagous insects that respond to specific host-plant chemicals (§6.8.3).

Most chemoreceptors, however, are generalists, responding differentially to a range of stimulus quality within their effective modality. This applies to most receptors for other modalities too. In such receptors, a given rate of firing can indicate the presence of either a low intensity of an effective stimulant or a high intensity

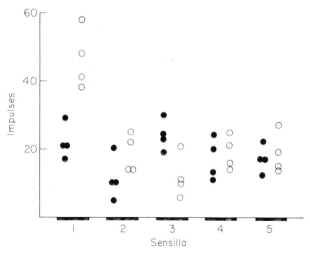

Fig. 4.8. Chemoreceptor functioning on the maxillary palps of locusts. The number of impulses occurring during the first second of four stimulations of five contact chemoreceptor sensilla with 'salt' ●, and four stimulations with 'fructose + salt' ○. Note the variability of response between stimulations with the same stimulant. Sensilla 4 and 5 show no particular sensitivity to either stimulant. Sensilla 2 and 3 are more sensitive to one stimulant than the other, but overlap occurs. Only sensillum 1 consistently allows distinction between the two (From data in Blaney, W. M. (1974) *J. exp. Biol.,* **62**, 555-569).

of a relatively ineffective stimulant. Such confusion is compounded with the variability inherent in all receptor systems (Fig. 4.8). The disadvantage of variability may be overcome by having many receptor cells in a given sense organ and averaging their output to improve the signal-to-noise ratio. Another advantage of multiple receptor systems is that they allow *range fractionation,* in which individual receptors respond to different parts of the range of stimulus intensity or quality covered by the whole organ. Thus in colour vision, receptor cells respond differentially but not exclusively to light of different wavelengths. The responses of generalist chemoreceptors are rather similar, in that a given receptor may respond maximally to a particular class of chemicals, but will respond to other chemicals too. The output from a given receptor is thus capable of several interpretations and an unambiguous assessment of the stimulus depends on an analysis in the CNS of the output from a number of receptors with different response characteristics.

Interneurones which receive inputs from receptors are almost always less numerous than the receptors themselves, and an important feature of coding is that they receive input from receptors having similar characteristics and therefore signalling the same 'message'. Thus, though stimulus information may first be coded in the receptor in analogue form, it reaches the CNS in digital form as spikes, in a code that may be comprehensible at the single cell level, but more usually is recognisable only in the simultaneous output of several receptors.

4.6   SYNAPTIC TRANSMISSION

4.6.1   Basic synaptic phenomena

Propagation of action potentials is interrupted at *synapses,* the points where one neurone contacts another or contacts a muscle cell. Transmission across a synapse is normally dependent on the diffusion across the synapse of a chemical released from the pre-synaptic cell. This chemical transmitter combines with receptor sites on the membrane of the post-synaptic cell and initiates a permeability change; the compound is inactivated by an enzyme which occurs in the membranes of both cells. At *excitatory synapses* this process, acting on the generator region of the post-synaptic cell, may be adequate to initiate an action potential. However, generally more than one pre-synaptic action potential is required to initiate a post-synaptic one (see § 4.7.2). At *inhibitory synapses,* the effect of synaptic transmission is to cause *hyper*polarization at the post-synaptic membrane rather than depolarization, thus lowering its chance of spiking.

Much of our knowledge of synaptic function derives from work on frogs. However, recent work on the terminal abdominal ganglion (A_6) of the cockroach, *Periplaneta,* particularly on the synapses between the sensory receptors on the anal cerci and the giant axons passing forwards to the thorax, has extended our knowledge to insects. Intracellular staining with procion yellow or cobalt chloride has revealed details of the highly complex arborizations of individual neurones from which electrical recordings have been made (Fig. 4.1), thus allowing a detailed correlation between neurophysiology and micro-anatomy.

Fig. 4.9. Post-synaptic responses recorded from cockroach A_6 ganglion. **A,** Biphasic PSP resulting from current pulse stimulation of the cercal nerve; a depolarizing component is followed by a hyperpolarizing component. **B,** Impulses in a cercal mechanoreceptor (upper trace) and corresponding EPSPs in a giant axon. **C,** Impulse in an unidentified cercal receptor and IPSP in A_6 ganglion. **D,** EPSPs resulting from electrical stimulation of the cercal nerve; the sub-threshold response (first trace) gives rise to an impulse (second trace) at slightly higher stimulation (After Callec, J. J. (1974) in *Insect Neurobiology,* ed. J. E. Treherne, North-Holland, Amsterdam, pp. 119-185).

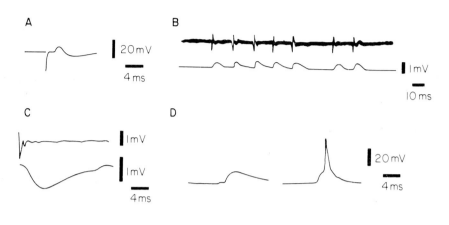

4.6.2   Post-synaptic responses

A post-synaptic change in membrane potential occurring in the CNS is called an excitatory post-synaptic potential (EPSP) if it is depolarizing, or an inhibitory post-synaptic potential (IPSP) if it is hyperpolarizing. In the cockroach A_6 ganglion preparation, stimulation of the whole cercal nerve by a current pulse evokes a biphasic post-synaptic potential in a giant axon, first depolarizing it, then hyperpolarizing it (Fig. 4.9A). A more precise analysis is obtained by stimulating a single mechanoreceptor on the cercus. The action potentials generated by it can be correlated with the resulting EPSPs recorded in the giant axon (Fig. 4.9B). Very light mechanical stimulation of the cercus may elicit IPSPs similar in form to the EPSPs but having a longer delay and, of course, opposite polarity (Fig. 4.9C). If the EPSP reaches an adequate amplitude, a propagated action potential is initiated (Fig. 4.9D). The biphasic response (Fig. 4.9A) probably results from the summation (§ 4.7.2) of an EPSP and an IPSP due to the stimulation of almost all the cercal receptor axons by the electrical pulse; the depolarization arrives first because the excitatory connections to the giant fibre are monosynaptic, whereas the inhibitory connections are bisynaptic, involving an intra-ganglionic neurone between the receptor and the giant fibre, and hence a delay.

4.6.3   The transmitter substance

A number of criteria must be met before a substance can be identified with confidence as a synaptic transmitter. It should be possible to identify the substance at the synapse and to demonstrate at the synaptic endings the presence of one enzyme for its synthesis and another for its inactivation. The substance should be released on stimulation and should be inhibited by competitive antagonists. It should also be possible to mimic the physiological action of the suspected transmitter by applying the chemical artificially in appropriate amounts. These criteria have not yet been rigorously satisfied for transmitters in the insect CNS but some progress has been made.

Acetylcholine (ACh) has been detected in the A_6 ganglion (§ 4.6.1) of the cockroach, but has not been localized in synaptic endings or in the intracellular vesicles associated with the pre-synaptic membrane. Its synthesizing enzyme, cholinacetylase, has been found only in whole ganglion preparations, but its inactivating enzyme, cholinesterase, has been located in synaptic regions. The esterase is inhibited by eserine, and in eserinized ganglia ACh has been shown to accumulate on stimulation. Synaptic transmission is blocked by application of d-tubocurarine and atropine, both competitors of ACh. Micro-injection of ACh produces post-synaptic depolarization with similar current-voltage properties to the normal EPSP. It thus appears likely that the main excitatory transmitter in the insect CNS is acetylcholine, but much of this evidence relates only to the A_6 ganglion of *Periplaneta,* and the existence of other excitatory transmitters is not excluded.

So far as an inhibitory transmitter is concerned, *gamma-aminobutyric acid* (GABA) appears to be a good candidate. It depresses electrical activity in the nervous system of several insects, occurs in the nerve cord of the cockroach and is taken up by cells in the cockroach brain. Although a GABA-synthesizing enzyme, glutamic acid decarboxylase, has been found, neither it nor GABA itself has yet been localized in the cockroach nervous system. No inactivating enzyme has yet been found, nor has production of GABA been shown to occur as a result of nerve stimulation. However, the action of naturally occurring GABA has been blocked in the cockroach A_6 ganglion by the inhibitor picrotoxin, and micro-injection of GABA can produce post-synaptic hyperpolarizations similar to the normal IPSPs. Thus, it is likely that GABA is a transmitter substance at inhibitory synapses, at least in the cockroach.

Work on the squid, indicates that Ca^{++} ions and perhaps Mg^{++} ions have a role in chemical transmissions at synapses. Although there is less evidence for this in insects, it is known that Ca^{++} ions are necessary for both excitatory and inhibitory transmission. By analogy with the squid work, it seems likely that Ca^{++} ions act on the transmitter release mechanism.

4.7 INTEGRATION

The coordination and control of cellular and organ function, including behaviour, is achieved by both neural and hormonal integration (see Chapters 3 and 6). Integration has occurred when an output is not identical to the input but is some function of it. It can occur at different levels within the nervous system. Incoming information, which may have been elaborately encoded (§4.5.3) by sensory neurones, must be decoded. The information may then be modified by interactions between different systems within the CNS. The principal mechanism is *synaptic integration*—the complex interactions that can occur between cells due to the

activity at synapses. The outcome of these processes may be long-lasting and result in learning (§6.5), or the information may be processed for immediate action. The output for action may be determined in part by a central programme, resulting from the characteristic activity of a group of interneurones (§4.7.4), and in part by peripheral feedback from receptors monitoring the effect of the output (§5.3). In either event, the outgoing commands are recoded to result in overt behavioural responses or internal regulative changes (§4.7.5).

4.7.1 Decoding

Our knowledge of decoding is sketchy but we have some information on the activity of identified interneurones responding to known input patterns from receptors. Recording the responses from olfactory sensilla on the antennae of *Periplaneta* has allowed the identification of seven generalist receptor neurone types (§4.5.3) each with different, but overlapping spectra of responsiveness to chemicals. The associated second-order neurones in the olfactory lobe of the brain consist of two types, one showing spontaneous activity, modulated in complex ways by input from antennal receptors which react to mechanical and thermal stimulation as well as to odours, and the other responding by excitation only, and only in response to odours. The response spectra of the latter for single compounds are wider than those of the peripheral receptor neurones, but for odours of potential foodstuffs, such as fruit and meat, they are more specific. The importance to the animal is obvious but the mechanism involved is not clear.

Similarly, in the auditory system of *Locusta,* four types of interneurone have been identified which respond in different ways to the input from auditory receptors stimulated by the species song, so that the combined response at the interneurone level allows all significant parameters of the song to be analyzed. Similar examples exist in the auditory systems of other Orthoptera and moths, where interneurones respond to biologically significant sound effects with greater specificity than can be found in peripheral receptors (Fig. 6.3D). Similar effects are achieved by visual interneurones which show preferential responses to movement of the whole visual field, or of objects within the field; in both cases there may be preferred directions of movement. Other visual interneurones respond to patterns or shapes, sometimes with a preferred orientation. Often the activity of these cells can be correlated with naturally occurring behavioural responses (e.g. optomotor orientation—Table 6.1).

4.7.2 Synaptic integration

Complex synaptic integration can be best understood by considering its various components separately.

Summation and facilitation

If post-synaptic potentials (PSPs) generated by the arrival of in-coming spikes from the pre-synaptic neurone overlap in time, they interact in two general forms. (1) *Summation,* when PSPs (see §4.6.1) arithmetically add to (if EPSPs) or subtract from (if IPSPs) the existing level of membrane depolarization. If the PSPs derive from different pre-synaptic neurones contacting the synapse, *spatial summation* is involved; if the PSPs derive from a single pre-synaptic neurone, *temporal summation* is involved. (2) *Facilitation,* this differs from summation in that successive PSPs are increased in amplitude as well as summed, so that the post-synaptic cell's membrane potential changes faster than it would by simple addition of the PSPs. Facilitation is probably a more common neural phenomenon than simple summation, but neither has been much explored in insects,

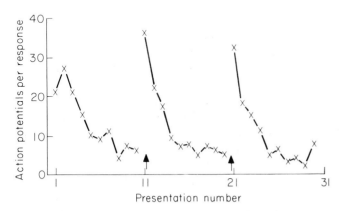

Fig. 4.10 Habituation and dishabituation in the response of a giant visual interneurone (the DCMD) in the locust. Each point represents the response when a 5° black disc is moved backward and forward horizontally, lateral to the animal's head, with an interstimulus interval of 10 s. Dishabituation occurs when the animal is rotated (at arrows) through 6° and 4° during an interstimulus interval (After Rowell, C. H. F. (1971) *J. exp. Biol.,* **55**, 749-761).

except in the terminal abdominal ganglion preparation in the cockroach (Fig. 4.9). Behaviourally, they are both usually loosely covered by the term 'summation' (§6.1.2).

Habituation

This occurs when a repeated stimulus of constant strength becomes progressively less effective so that the strength or frequency of the behavioural response gradually decreases (§6.1.3). It has been studied neurophysiologically in the descending contralateral movement detector (DCMD) of the locust. This is a large visual interneurone associated with each compound eye. It is especially sensitive to movements of small objects stimulating only part of the retina. With repeated stimulation, habituation soon occurs and may last for several hours. If, however, the locust is moved slightly so that the stimulus affects a different part of the eye, immediate *dishabituation* occurs and the response then rehabituates (Fig. 4.10). When dishabituation occurs, the previous stimulus is once again effective, so that habituation and dishabituation must occur at different loci within the nervous system. When the animal itself moves, dishabituation is somehow prevented, even though the stimulation of the retina must have changed. Thus, for example, during antennal cleaning, in which the insect moves its head around all three major axes by up to 25°, there is no dishabituation of DCMD response. This is not due to inhibition of DCMD response during cleaning, because if a new visual stimulus is presented, full DCMD response is obtained; it is only with 'familiar' stimuli which have already produced habituation that dishabituation is prevented. To recognise movement of 'familiar' stimuli on the retina, the insect must take account of movement of the head. This is not done simply by proprioception because experimentally applied passive movement of the head does not produce the same effect; it must also involve analysis of motor output, probably to the neck muscles. In this way, selective attention to significant features of the environment may be achieved.

4.7.3 Learning

Behavioural experiments leave no doubt that learning occurs in some insects (§6.5), but investigation of the neurophysiology of learning has so far been unrewarding.

4.7.4   Central or peripheral control?

Commonly, parts of the CNS, especially the brain, exert an inhibitory effect on other parts.   Thus, in the grasshopper, *Gastrimargus,* decapitation results in an increase in the responsiveness and a decline in the rate of habituation of auditory interneurones (Fig. 4.11). Similar inhibitory control may be exercised by the sub-oesophageal ganglion; its removal in male mantids and cockroaches leads to increased spike activity in the phallic nerve and repeated attempts at copulation (§6.1.4).   Conversely, lesions of the CNS may reduce excitability.

Changes in responsiveness also occur in the intact insect; stimuli which would normally produce a response often fail to do so during mating or cryptic behaviour. Conversely, the blowfly, *Phormia,* fails to respond to stimulation of a single labellar chemoreceptor with water when the fly is water-satiated, but does respond if an adjacent chemoreceptor is briefly stimulated with sugar just before the water stimulation (§6.1.4). Neurophysiological recording of these chemoreceptors shows that (a) the water receptor fires at the same rate before and after the sugar stimulation, and (b) input from the sugar receptor has ceased before the second water stimulation.   Clearly, a heightened level of

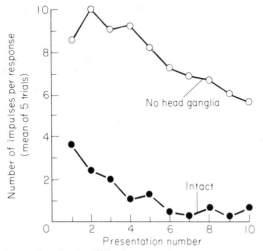

Fig. 4.11. The change in responsiveness of an auditory inter-neurone in the grasshopper, *Gastrimargus,* before and after decapitation (After Rowell, C. H. F. (1970) in *Short-term Changes in Neural Activity and Behaviour*; Eds: G. Horne & R. A. Hinde, Cambridge Univ. Press).

excitability has occurred, and persisted, within the CNS. In addition to this *central excitatory state,* a separate central inhibitory state is believed to occur in the CNS of the blowfly (§6.1.4).

There is ample evidence that the output of motor neurones involved in ventilation, flight, stridulation and walking is organized, at least partly, by *central nervous generators* (see Fig. 4.12). Although not yet identified, the generators are believed to be endogenously active neurones generating a rhythmically varying output. At least two principles operate to prevent the insect from carrying out all its rhythmically-driven activities simultaneously: the endogenously active neurones can be inhibited by other cells, and they may need an excitatory input from other systems to start them functioning. Reliance on central programmes ensures a fixed output which is useful in many activities and economical of neurones, but does not allow flexibility or compensation for injury. However, although the programme for flight activity can be generated in the absence of sensory input, it is capable of considerable modification in response to sensory feedback (§5.3.1). Indeed it seems probable that no behavioural programme, however simple, is uninfluenced by the sensory feedback it generates, and in more complex behaviour, many more modifying influences operate in the CNS (§6.1).

4.7.5   Recoding

The recoding of information into spike sequences to act as commands to motor organs (mainly muscles) is influenced by the relatively small number of neurones at the insect's disposal, and by the complex ways in which the neuromuscular systems operate to achieve considerable diversity of function (see §5.3).

4.8   NEUROSECRETION

Almost all neurones influence other neurones or muscle cells by the secretion of chemicals at specialized regions, usually at or near the ends of axons (§4.6.3). That is to say, virtually all neurones are capable of secretion. In the majority of neurones, the released secretion is only effective at the synapse in which it is released and the duration of its effectiveness is very short. By contrast, the chemicals released by neurosecretory cells can be long-lasting and may be released into the haemolymph to circulate as true hormones (§3.3.1); that is, the gap between the pre- and post-synaptic membranes may be very large.

4.8.1　Form and occurrence of neurosecretory cells

Most neurosecretory cells are monopolar neurones whose axon gives off one or more branched colaterals near to the cell body. It is through synapses in these dendritic colaterals that the neurone is stimulated by neighbouring neurones. The axon has terminal branches ending in bulbous regions which either lie between the perineurium and neural lamella (p. 55), if their contents are to be dispersed into the haemolymph, or may invade a target organ directly. The neurosecretory material, synthesized in the cell body, is transported along the axon in membrane-bound vesicles which often accumulate in large numbers in the terminal swellings.

Neurosecretory cells occur both in peripheral nerves and in the CNS, where their cell bodies can be found in all the ganglia (Fig. 3.2). The axonal endings of those in the CNS are usually found in discrete *neurohaemal organs* (e.g. the corpora cardiaca—§3.3.1) which sometimes occur as segmentally arranged swellings on the sympathetic nervous system. Neurosecretory cells in the peripheral nerves utilize the same neurohaemal organs, or have their endings more widely scattered about the peripheral nervous system.

4.8.2　Functioning and control of neurosecretory cells

Neurosecretory cells appear to function similarly to other neurones; the release of neurosecretion resembles the release of synaptic transmitter, and stimulation of the dendritic areas by other neurones may be either excitatory or inhibitory. In some neurosecretory cells of the stick insect, Ca^{++} acts as the major carrier of inward current in the action potential recorded from the cell body. It may be that this is a general feature of insect neurosecretory cells. Action potentials in neurosecretory cells have a time course of about 5 ms, rather than the 1 ms typical of normal neurones, and this may be related to the time needed for the release of neurosecretory granules, which are substantially larger than the vesicles of synaptic transmitter. Reduction of Ca^{++} in the bathing medium diminishes the release of neurosecretion, and it is assumed, by analogy with other animals, that on depolarization of the axon terminal by the action potential, Ca^{++} enters the cell and facilitates release of neurosecretory vesicles.

Immediate control of neurosecretion results from the synaptic activity of other neurones but it may be assumed that these, in turn, are controlled either by input from external receptors responding to features of the environment, or by input from internal receptors monitoring the internal environment of the insect.

4.8.3　Hormones affecting neural activity

Hormones affect behaviour in a variety of ways (§6.4), and must therefore affect neural functioning. When tested on nerve preparations, hormones are found to cause profound changes in spontaneous neural activity, switching on or off particular programmes or modifying existing activity. For example, injection of extracts of the corpora cardiaca (CC) into male cockroaches produces neural activity in their phallic nerves, correlated with copulatory movements similar to those induced by decapitation (§4.7.4, §6.1.4). Apparently the hormone acts on the sub-oesophageal ganglion to remove its inhibition of the abdominal motor centres.

The eclosion hormone found in the brain and CC of pharate silkmoths releases a pre-patterned programme of behaviour which enables the emerging adult to escape from the pupal cuticle and cocoon (§7.4). This behaviour involves first some 30 min of rotational movements of the abdomen, then, after a rest, a further 30 min of anterior-moving abdominal peristaltic waves, which culminate in emergence. If the source of the hormone is absent, as in isolated abdomens, the behaviour does not normally occur, but injection of homogenates of brain and CC into such abdomens, releases the full eclosion behaviour. Furthermore, completely isolated abdominal nerve cords respond to eclosion hormone by producing a motor output appropriate for the behaviour observed in the intact insect (Fig. 4.12). The motor programme for this activity is therefore built into the abdominal nerve cord and is normally switched on by eclosion hormone.

It is not necessary for the hormone to be present throughout the behavioural response, however, because the correct sequence of the two active phases is determined by the latency with which each responds to the hormonal trigger. The two phases are further controlled by separate neuronal circuits each having two elements:

Fig. 4.12. The motor activity of an isolated abdominal nerve cord of a pupal silkmoth in response to eclosion hormone. A, B, C, recording sites (simultaneous records at right); G_2, G_3, second and third ganglia. The records represent the integrated neural activity (occurring in typical bursts) during two active phases. During the first phase, characterized by rotational movements of the abdomen, there is a right-left alternation of output (cf. timing of A and B). During the second phase, when peristaltic movements occur, bilateral bursts are recorded, beginning in the more posterior ganglion and proceeding anteriorly (cf. timing of C *versus* A and B) (After Truman, J. W. & Riddiford, L. M. (1974) Hormonal mechanisms underlying insect behaviour. *Adv. Insect Physiol.,* **10**, 297-352).

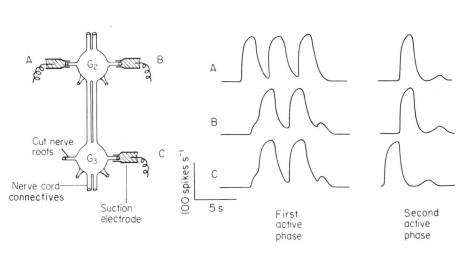

a 'burst timer', which determines the inter-burst intervals, and a 'burst pattern generator', which determines the nature of the neural output within each burst (see also §4.7.4, §5.3).

Besides switching on eclosion behaviour, the same hormone switches on adult motor patterns such as flight, and shortly after eclosion switches off the motor neurones innervating the abdominal muscles used during eclosion; thereafter these muscles degenerate rapidly.

4.9   INSECTICIDES

Most of the early insecticides were stomach poisons and were selective for plant pest species; parasites, predators or species which did not ingest the plant were not killed. However, in those insects which ate the sprayed leaves, free toxins would be liberated within the gut. Insecticides at present in common use disrupt the functioning of the nervous system and are used as a residual film deposited on the plant surface. Uptake of the insecticide can be over the whole surface of the insect or by mouth. To be effective by surface penetration, the insecticides have to be sufficiently lipophilic to permeate the cuticular waxes or the epicuticular lining of the tracheal system. The first insecticides to act in this way were the organochlorines (Fig. 4.13) such as DDT, Dieldrin and BHC. These compounds are potent insecticides, but are not highly toxic toward man. Organochlorines, or their degradative products, may be extremely persistent in the environment and accumulate within food chains. However, in controlled usage they can give non-hazardous, long-lasting and inexpensive control of many pests.

In recent years, organochlorines have become restricted in use and organophosphates and carbamates (Fig. 4.13) are now employed extensively. Pyrethroids (Fig. 4.13) have exciting possibilities as pesticides but are only now attaining wide commercial use. The modes of action of these compounds are discussed in §4.9.2-4.9.6. The carbamates and organophosphates are effective poisons and have a distinct advantage in that they can act systemically as well as by contact. In *systemic* effects the compounds are absorbed through the leaves and roots and become distributed in a general way throughout the plant. This may overcome any uneven initial application of pesticide and moreover ensure contamination of plant parts which grow after the initial application. Such uptake ensures that systemic compounds will be effective against aphids and other insects that feed on sap.

Pyrethrum is the only naturally occurring insecticide in common use. Synthetic pyrethroids with enhanced insecticidal activity are being developed (§4.9.6); their major advantage is their low mammalian toxicity,

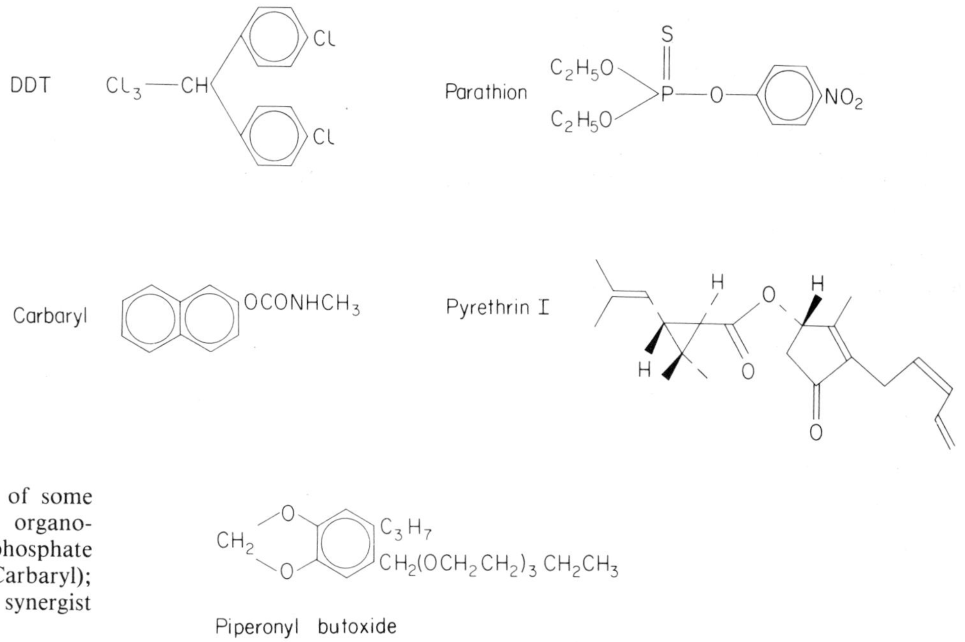

Fig. 4.13. Chemical structure of some typical synthetic insecticides: organochlorine (DDT); organophosphate (Parathion); carbamate (Carbaryl); pyrethroid (Pyrethrin I) and a synergist (Piperonyl butoxide).

whereas both carbamates and organophosphates are highly toxic to mammals and other vertebrates.

4.9.1 Synergists and insecticide detoxification

Pesticide synergists are compounds that have negligible toxicity at doses employed in the field but which enhance markedly the toxicity of a pesticide. The synergist is often applied in conjunction with the pesticide but many are effective if applied some time prior to the application of the pesticide. Synergists were developed originally to increase the toxicity of natural pyrethrins and so reduce the cost of control measures. They are now available not only for pyrethroids but also for nicotine, organochlorines, organophosphates and carbamates. In field use, synergists are employed only in combination with pyrethroids. Synergists are restricted in use primarily because of technical problems. They differ both physically and chemically from the pesticide and this poses problems in keeping the two chemicals together under field conditions.

It is difficult to give a comprehensive account of all synergists, but a typical one is shown in Fig. 4.13. In general they act by interfering with the detoxification of the insecticide, though they may also facilitate its pene-

tration. A major enzyme complex involved in insecticide detoxification is the mixed function oxidase system; this system is involved in the inactivation of pyrethrins, organochlorines, organophosphates and carbamates and may be blocked by the synergists. Some synergists block esterase and epoxide hydrase; esterases are important in the detoxification of some synthetic pyrethroids, while both esterase and epoxide hydrase are responsible for the deactivation of compounds related to juvenile hormone (Fig. 3.11). It is of interest that piperonyl butoxide has juvenilizing effects when applied on its own; such an effect is due probably to an enhancement of the titre of endogenous juvenile hormone within the insect, caused by inhibition of enzymic deactivation of the hormone by the synergist.

4.9.2 Effects on axonal transmission

DDT appears to bind to the axon membrane and to interfere with the flow of ions into and out of the axon. An analysis of the ion movements in DDT-poisoned axons, and a knowledge of the three-dimensional structure of the DDT molecule suggests that the wide base of the molecule combines with the membrane protein, while its narrower apex keeps open a 'gate' for sodium ions in the lipid part of the membrane. It is envisaged that the potassium gates are also affected, accounting for the sustained increase in potassium conductance of the membrane. The effect of these permeability changes is that DDT causes repetitive production of action potentials. In the poisoned insect, this results in hyper-excitability and muscular spasms, followed by paralysis and death. Unless the lethal effect is rapid, the early symptoms are soon overtaken by a generalized stress syndrome. Blood from a cockroach in this condition may cause death when injected into an untreated cockroach, a toxic effect probably due to the massive release of neurosecretion (see §4.9.5).

4.9.3   Effects on the acetylcholine receptor

Some insecticides, including nicotine, act by combining with the acetylcholine receptor sites on the postsynaptic membrane. Nicotine, and those of its analogues which show insecticidal action, all share certain structural similarities with acetylcholine. Nicotine will bind with ACh-receptor protein extracted from housefly heads, and there is good correlation between the degree of binding of nicotine and its analogues, and their varying toxicities in the intact animal. Application of a lethal dose produces tremors, convulsions and then paralysis, with death usually occurring within the hour.

4.9.4   Effects on acetylcholinesterase

Organophosphorus and carbamate insecticides inhibit the action of acetylcholinesterase. The proposed mechanism of action for acetylcholinesterase in insects is shown in Fig. 4.14. Evidence from biochemical studies suggests that the inhibition produced by the

organophosphates and carbamates is due to their similarity to acetylcholine and their ability to react with the esterase in the same way as the normal substrate. The effectiveness of the inhibitors results from the relatively long life of the phosphorylated or carbamyl-ated enzyme compared with the acetylated enzyme of the normal reaction. The result of inhibition of the enzyme is the build up of acetylcholine at the synapses and the development of prolonged EPSPs. Initially, the poisoned insect shows hyperactivity, then lack of co-ordination, paralysis and finally death.

4.9.5   Effects on neurosecretion

A variety of insecticides, including the organo-phosphates, the carbamates and DDT, disrupt the functioning of the neurosecretory system to cause the release of diuretic hormone (§2.4.1), cuticle plasticizing factor, hyperglycaemic factors and adipokinetic hormone pp. 10 and 11). Thus insecticides may kill, either by a direct effect on the nervous system itself, or by this secondary effect of release of excessive amounts of neurohormones, depending on the species of insect and its physiological state at the time of poisoning.

4.9.6   Mode of action of pyrethroids

Pyrethroids (Fig. 4.13) exhibit two distinct effects upon insects, one is lethal and the other is the so called 'knock down' action. In spite of the fact that natural pyrethrum has been known as a potent insecticide for more than a century, there is still much to be elucidated concerning its insecticidal effects. Vertebrate nerves are relatively insensitive to pyrethrins applied directly. However, in insects the pyrethrins combine with the lipids in the

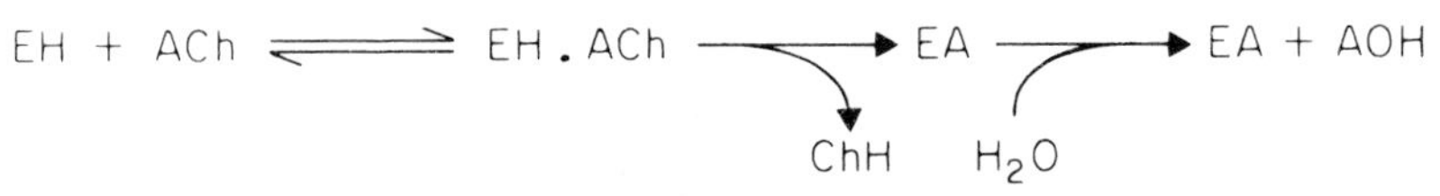

Fig. 4.14. A proposed mechanism of action for the enzyme acetylcholinester-ase. EH = the enzyme, ACh = acetyl-choline, EH.ACh = reversible complex between enzyme and substrate, EA = acetylated enzyme, ChH = choline, AOH = acetic acid. Hydrolysis of the acetylated enzyme to release the original free enzyme occurs much more rapidly than hydrolysis of the phosphorlyated or carbamylated enzyme formed by insecti-cide action (see Corbett, J. R. (1974) *The Biochemical Mode of Action of Pesticides.* Academic Press, London).

$$EH + ACh \rightleftharpoons EH.ACh \longrightarrow EA \longrightarrow EA + AOH$$

$$ChH \qquad H_2O$$

nerve cell membranes and disrupt cationic conductance. Such effects can lead to increased excitation of the nervous system, which induces 'knock down', and to paralysis caused by a block in the nerves at the cellular and peripheral levels. Insects can recover from knock down, and from paralysis, by the detoxification of the pyrethroid; obviously permanent damage is not done to the nervous system. The lethal effects of pyrethrins are due to lesions in tissues other than nerves, but this effect is poorly understood. The two effects are not necessarily linked and some pyrethroids are strongly insecticidal but exhibit poor knock down.

Further reading

Aidley D. J. (1971) *The Physiology of Excitable Cells.* Cambridge University Press, London.

Bullock T. H., Orkand R. & Grinnell A. (1977) *Introduction to Nervous Systems.* W. H. Freeman & Co., San Francisco.

Miller P. L. (1974) The neural basis of behaviour. In *Insect Neurobiology* (Ed. J. E. Treherne). North-Holland, Amsterdam.

Chapter 5
Muscles and Movement

Muscles are biological machines which convert chemical energy into mechanical work and into heat. Skeletal muscles in insects are attached at both ends to the cuticle and usually extend across a flexible region or a joint. Contraction of the muscle causes one part of the skeleton, on which the muscle is said to be inserted, to move towards a less mobile part, on which the muscle is said to have its origin. Since muscles only do useful work on contraction, skeletal muscles normally occur in antagonistic pairs or groups, one of which reverses the action of the other. The circular and longitudinal coats of visceral muscle surrounding the soft organs of the body also act as antagonists. Throughout the animal kingdom there is a common basis of contractility; the machinery consists of mainly fibrous proteins, principally myosin and actin, and the ultimate fuel is ATP (§1.3).

5.1 MUSCLE STRUCTURE

Muscle is made up from smaller sub-units, the *fibres,* which are its physiological units, each derived from several cells (Fig. 5.1). The fibre is made up from rods of protein, the *fibrils,* which run the length of it. Each fibril is divided longitudinally into many segments or *sarcomeres* by partitions, the Z discs, which may be aligned on adjacent fibrils so that the whole fibre has a striated appearance (Fig. 5.2). It is believed that all insect muscle is striated, but the lateral register of adjacent fibrils may be so poor that banding is not seen in the fibre as a whole. Within each fibril there are interdigitating thick and thin filaments, composed of the proteins myosin and actin respectively (Fig. 5.2). According to the sliding filament theory, contraction results from the myosin and actin filaments sliding past each other, without themselves decreasing in length, and bringing successive Z discs closer together with a resulting overall shortening of the muscle.

Various types of muscle occur in insects but only flight muscles will be considered here, since they are so characteristic of insects and have been well studied. On structural grounds, three broad categories of flight muscle are normally recognized, *tubular, close-packed* and *fibrillar* (Fig. 5.1). Functionally, they fall into two distinct groups, *synchronous* (non-fibrillar) muscle, to which the tubular and close-packed types belong, and *asynchronous* muscle to which the fibrillar type belongs. In the former, there is a 1:1 ratio between the occurrence of motor nerve impulses and mechanical responses, whereas in the latter the frequency of contraction is

Fig. 5.1. Types of skeletal muscle fibre found in insects. **A,** Tubular: the central column of nuclei is surrounded by radially disposed, alternating rows of fibrils and mitochondria. **B,** Close-packed: the nuclei are peripheral and the small fibrils are interspersed with columns of large mitochondria. **C,** Fibrillar: the large fibrils are cylindrical and separated by columns of mitochondria; the nuclei (not shown) are peripheral. N, nucleus; F, fibrils; M, mitochondria; S, sarcomere (After Wigglesworth V. B. (1972) *Principles of Insect Physiology,* 7e Chapman & Hall).

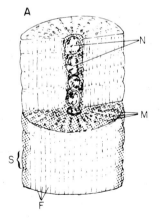 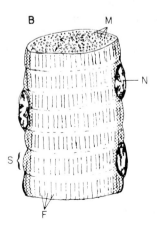 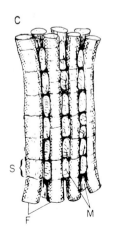

A

B

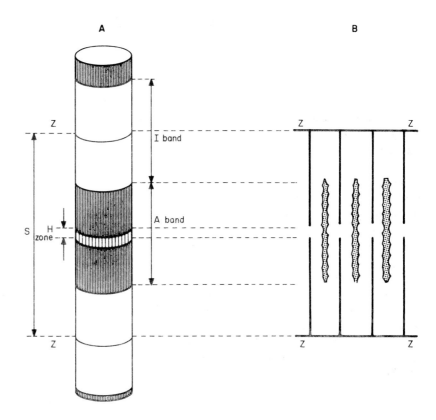

Fig. 5.2. Diagrammatic representation of a single fibril **A**, showing a sarcomere (S) delimited by Z discs (Z) and identifying the I band (I), A band (A) and H zone (H). Diagram **B**, shows the disposition of actin filaments (thin lines) and myosin filaments (stippled lines) within a sarcomere and shows their relationship to the banding pattern.

much greater than, and not closely related to, the frequency of nerve impulses.

5.1.1 Fine structure of muscles

Most of our detailed information derives from studies on the flight muscles of the blowfly, *Calliphora,* and the giant water bug, *Lethocercus.* The unit of length between Z discs on a fibril, the sarcomere, is found to consist mainly of myosin and actin filaments disposed as shown in Fig. 5.2. Each myosin filament is surrounded by six actin filaments giving a double hexagonal array in cross-section. The myosin filaments are long coiled chains of polypeptides, and the actin filaments are coiled double strands of globular proteins. In *Lethocercus,* both types of filament are double helices, the myosin filaments being left-handed and the actin filaments right-handed. Except in their central region, the myosin filaments have lateral projections, called cross-bridges, which interact with the actin filaments to develop the force for contraction. The presence of other structural proteins,

tropomyosin, troponin A and troponin B, is inferred from work on vertebrate muscle, and from experiments on the calcium-sensitizing system in insect muscle (§5.2.2).

There are suggestions from the ultrastructure that two other types of filament also occur. Thin filaments, called T-filaments run parallel to the actin and myosin filaments and link the Z discs; their elasticity could account for the residual tension in muscles which have been extended to a point where no overlap remains between the actin and myosin filaments. A similar function has been ascribed to the C-filaments believed to link the ends of the myosin filaments to the Z disc.

The precise nature of the Z disc is unclear. In some insect fibrils, no apparent structure can be seen in the disc, but in others fine filaments are apparent, sometimes as a dense mass, sometimes with a basket-weave appearance. As the actin and myosin filaments slide past each other during contraction, the Z discs could impose a limit on the extent of shortening possible.

However, there is good evidence that in many visceral, cardiac and larval skeletal muscles *supercontraction* occurs, in which filaments penetrate from their sarcomere of origin, through the Z disc, into the adjacent sarcomere.

Skeletal muscles are attached to the cuticle via epidermal cells. From the Z discs of the terminal sarcomeres, attachment filaments extend to the cell boundaries between the muscle and epidermal cells where desmosomes occur. From these, microtubules run in the epidermal cells to end in hemidesmosomes under pore canals in the cuticle (Fig. 2.13). Attachment fibres run in the pore canals to the epicuticle. Thus, there are no tendons.

At frequent intervals the plasma membrane surrounding the fibre is invaginated to form the T-tubules which penetrate deep into the fibres (Fig. 5.3). Closely associated with these tubules is the *sarcoplasmic reticulum* (SR), a system of tubules and vesicles having no direct connection with the outer membrane of the muscle. The SR serves to control contraction by regulating the availability of Ca^{++} ions to the actin/myosin complex (§1.3.1; §5.2.2).

5.1.2 Innervation and the nerve-muscle synapse

The fibres of insect skeletal muscles are normally controlled by several motor neurones, which may come from different body segments. In addition to this polyneurony, the innervation is multiterminal, each neurone branching and making many points of contact with the muscle (Fig. 5.3). In the femoral part of the retractor unguis muscle in the hind leg of the locust, *Schistocerca gregaria,* the two motor neurones which innervate the muscle each have between 4000 and 5000 axon terminals. Each terminal, 15-30 μm in length, has 5-30 synaptic areas so that the muscle has about 100 000 synaptic contacts from the two motor neurones. It should be emphasized that the insect muscle cell membrane, in contrast to that of vertebrates, does not propagate action potentials, hence the need for synapses every 100 μm or so. Three classes of motor neurone occur in the innervation of most insects, *fast* and *slow* excitatory neurones, and *inhibitory* neurones, and by their combined effects they can achieve considerable sophistication of control with relatively few neurones (§5.3.2).

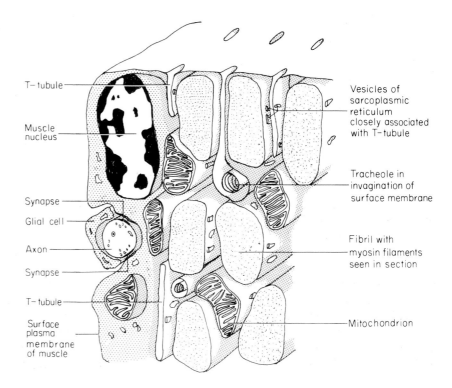

Fig. 5.3. Transverse section and three-dimensional arrangement of part of an insect flight muscle fibre. Note the effectively 'intra-cellular' nature of the tracheal supply and the multiple synapses (of which only two are shown) between each motor axon and muscle cell (After Pringle J. W. S. (1975) *Insect Flight* Oxford Biology Readers 52. Oxford University Press).

T-tubule

Muscle nucleus

Synapse

Glial cell

Axon

Synapse

T-tubule

Surface plasma membrane of muscle

Vesicles of sarcoplasmic reticulum closely associated with T-tubule

Tracheole in invagination of surface membrane

Fibril with myosin filaments seen in section

Mitochondrion

Axons may synapse with projections from the muscle cell, lie in a groove in the surface of the cell, or extend deeper into the cell to become enclosed by it. In all cases, the axonal glial sheath (§4.2) is absent from the synaptic surfaces and in these regions of the axon large numbers of spherical, electron-transparent synaptic vesicles occur (§4.6.3).

5.2 MUSCLE FUNCTIONING

Neuromuscular synapses are thought to work in much the same way as interneuronal synapses (§4.6). Each action potential causes the release of transmitter which opens ion gates in the muscle membrane and the resultant current flow is either depolarizing (at excitatory synapses) or hyperpolarizing (at inhibitory synapses). Depolarizing currents affect the permeability of adjacent regions so that the effect spreads and, via the T-tubule system, reaches the interior of the muscle and activates the contraction mechanism (§5.2.2). Hyperpolarizing currents reduce the depolarizing effect of excitatory synapses and inhibit contraction.

5.2.1 The nerve-muscle synapse

It is now accepted that *L-glutamate* acts as the excitatory transmitter in many insect somatic muscles and that *gamma-aminobutyric acid* (GABA) is probably the principal inhibitory transmiter (cf. §4.6.3). The number of muscle systems investigated so far is limited, however.

Micro-application of L-glutamate to the muscle has shown that high sensitivity is restricted to localized spots on the membrane. Presumably these are the synpatic regions; peak contraction force is proportional to the concentration of glutamate applied. A possible glutamate receptor protein has been isolated from locust muscle and found to have a high affinity for L-glutamate but a low affinity for L-aspartate and L-glutamine. These results agree well with pharmacological studies on the intact muscle. L-glutamate causes desensitization of synaptic receptors, resulting in a reduction in impulse-linked depolarization, but it does not abolish either neural conduction or the electrical excitability of the muscle. Thus, it is unlikely that the artificially applied L-glutamate is acting pre-synaptically

to cause the release of the 'real' excitatory transmitter. Amino acids other than L-glutamate (e.g. D-glutamate or L-aspartate) will also cause insect muscle to contract, though less efficiently. This lack of strict specificity suggests that the muscle membrane interacts weakly with many molecules whose stereochemistry is similar to that of L-glutamate, but that the result is a less efficient change of membrane permeability.

Two intriguing questions remain. First, there exist on the muscle membrane extra-synaptic sites which are sensitive to L-glutamate and respond either by depolarization or by hyperpolarization, but whose function is unknown. Second, insect blood contains more than enough L-glutamate to activate the muscles, but does not do so. Possibly synpases in deep-seated clefts are protected from the blood-borne glutamate; alternatively, synapses may be protected by a physical barrier such as the glial cells (since muscle is less sensitive to L-glutamate in the intact insect than when dissected out) (cf. §4.4); or possibly much of the blood glutamate may be held, for example, in haemocytes, so that it cannot act on the synpases. The complete answer to the anomaly is not known.

Unlike L-glutamate, GABA occurs in small quantities in insect nervous tissue and is known to act as a transmitter in other animal groups. Most of the work in insects has been carried out on locusts, in which application of GABA increases the permeability of muscle fibres to Cl⁻ and causes hyperpolarization. GABA is effective only in those somatic muscles which have an inhibitory innervation and the response occurs only at inhibitory synapses.

Transmitters can be removed from the neuromuscular synapse in three ways: by simple diffusion, enzymic degradation, or active uptake by neighbouring cells. Only in a few synapses could diffusion be fast enough to account for the short-lived pulse, and enzymic degradation of L-glutamate at synapses has not yet been shown convincingly. However, experiments with radio-labelled glutamate have shown that it is taken up actively into glial cells around the synapse, and to a lesser extent into the axons and muscle cells. The glial cells may act as a store for L-glutamate, allowing it to be translocated to the axons as needed. Similar results for GABA have been found in Crustacea but not yet in insects, though it is likely that both groups use the same system.

5.2.2   Excitation-contraction coupling

Events linking depolarization and muscle contraction in insects are not well understood because of the small size of insect muscles and their fibres, and the extent to which they resist separation due to the enmeshing tracheal system. However, the existing evidence fits well with what is known of the corresponding mechanisms in vertebrate and crustacean striated muscle.

Raising the external K^+ concentration is a convenient way of causing depolarization in muscle and can be used to show that a graded tension develops in the muscle related to the degree of depolarization. In frog and crab muscle, the depolarization spreads to the interior of the fibres by the T-tubule system. The T-system is well developed in insects (Fig. 5.3) and is believed to fulfil the same function, although direct evidence is lacking. Work on vertebrates has shown that depolarization of the T-system causes the release of Ca^{++} from the sarcoplasmic reticulum (SR), and the Ca^{++} ions are believed to activate the actomyosin Mg-ATPase, resulting in sliding of the actin and myosin filaments past each other and thus contraction of the muscle fibre. The involvement of Ca^{++} in contraction in insects has been shown in locust leg muscle. If perfused for 30 min with a calcium-free solution (containing the calcium-chelating agent EDTA) the muscle will no longer contract in response to applied K^+, but if calcium chloride is then added, the capacity to contract is restored. SR isolated from homogenized locust flight muscle can bind Ca^{++} in the presence of ATP, and will inhibit muscle ATPase. Thus there is good evidence that in insects, as in vertebrates, calcium ions are involved in contraction and that the SR can sequester these ions by means of an ATP-driven pump. The precise mechanism of Ca^{++} release from SR is not known, but the close association between T-tubules and SR may produce a low resistance pathway, and depolarization spreading to the SR vesicles may alter the permeability of the latter to Ca^{++}.

The role of Ca^{++} in activating Mg-ATPase, with consequent activation of crossbridges between actin and myosin, is under the control of several other proteins known collectively as 'native tropomyosin', which includes tropomyosin and troponin A and B. The role of these in the operation of the sliding filament mecha-

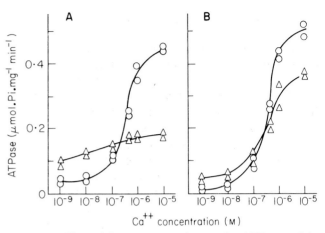

Fig. 5.4. Effect of Ca^{++} concentration on the ATPase activity of myofibrils of **A**, honey-bee and **B**, locust. $\triangle$, flight muscle; $\bigcirc$, leg muscle; Pi, inorganic phosphate. The fibrillar flight muscle from the honey-bee is less sensitive than the other muscles (From Aidley, D. J. (1975) in *Insect Muscle*, ed. Usherwood, P. N. R., Academic Press, London, pp. 337-356).

nism in vertebrates is believed to be as follows: troponin inhibits the actin-myosin interaction and tropomyosin makes that inhibition dependent on Ca^{++}; release of Ca^{++} from SR removes the inhibition of the actin-myosin-ATP interaction and contraction occurs.

Evidence for the occurrence of such a system in insect muscle is sparse and indirect. The myofibrillar fraction of homogenized insect muscle will split Mg-ATP in solutions containing KCl and Ca^{++} ions, and the degree of ATPase activity is dependent on the Ca^{++} concentration (Fig. 5.4). The action of trypsin on actomyosin or myofibril preparations from the water bug, *Lethocercus,* is to reduce the control which Ca^{++} concentration exerts on ATPase activity so that high levels of ATPase activity occur at all Ca^{++} concentrations. If, however, native tropomyosin from rabbit skeletal muscle is added, to replace that digested by the trypsin, the sensitivity to calcium returns.

Asynchronous (fibrillar—§5.1) flight muscle from a number of insects is less sensitive to Ca^{++} concentration than synchronous flight muscle or other skeletal muscle (Fig. 5.4). This feature of asynchronous muscle is correlated with reduced development of SR. The functional significance is not clear but it may allow finer control of contraction than is possible with the more steeply sigmoidal relationship found with the other muscles.

5.3 MUSCLES AND LOCOMOTION

A major function of skeletal muscle is to provide the forces necessary for locomotion. All insect locomotion involves the reciprocating action of pairs or groups of muscles acting antagonistically. Muscles may act directly on the appendages to move them against the substrate or surrounding medium and so produce locomotion. Alternatively, they may act indirectly by altering the shape of parts of the body to which the appendages are attached. Muscles involved in locomotion can show considerable variability in function: the same muscle may fulfil two different roles at different times (e.g. in flight and in walking; corresponding muscles on opposite sides of the body may contract together in flight but be out of phase in walking).

Since locomotion involves rhythmically repeated sequences of activity, it could theoretically be regulated entirely by the interaction between peripheral sensory feedback systems; each step or wingbeat could provide the input necessary to initiate the next. Sense organs do provide appropriate information for this to happen, but there is evidence also for the occurrence of rhythmical activity, either of neurones, e.g. in cockroach walking (§5.3.2) or of muscles, e.g. in blowfly flight (§5.3.1), which is independent of immediate sensory feedback.

These mechanisms can be initiated and persist even with sensory feedback totally removed (§6.1.5), and in intact insects there are situations when sensory feedback is apparently ignored. Nevertheless, it seems that in most cases, realization of the full potential for controlled locomotion requires peripheral monitoring of the results of locomotor activity, including the effects of changes which the insect 'intended' to make and changes forced upon it, and the utilization of that information to adjust the overall motor output. These and other principles are best illustrated by reference to particular modes of locomotion.

5.3.1 Flight

Wing movement depends on the action of muscles either acting directly, by pulling on the wing bases, or indirectly, by altering the shape of the thorax. The upbeat of the wings is caused by the indirect, dorso-ventral muscles which pull down the top of the thorax, which in turn forces the wings upwards (Fig. 5.5 A(i), B(i)). In more primitive insects (e.g. Odonata, Blattaria) downbeat is caused by direct muscles inserted onto the base of the wings (Fig. 5.5A(iii)). In Diptera and Hymenoptera, indirect muscles, running the length of the thorax, distort the shape of the thoracic box, raising its top,

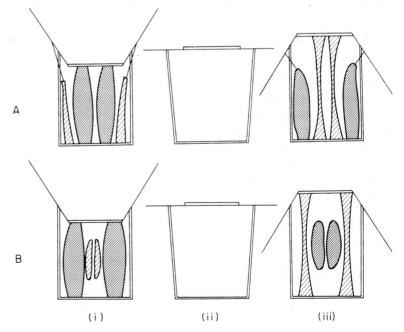

Fig. 5.5. Diagrammatic representation of a transverse section through the thorax of an insect such as a dragonfly **A**, and a housefly **B**, to show the changing shape of the thorax and position of the wings as the principal flight muscles are contracted (heavy shading) and relaxed (light shading). The intermediate position (ii) is unstable, having at least four points of articulation in a row subject to lateral and vertical stresses. From this, the wings readily click into the up (i) or down (iii) position.

A

B

(i)   (ii)   (iii)

which forces the wings downwards (Fig. 5.5 B(iii)). Other orders use a combination of direct and indirect muscles on the downbeat. Because of the stiffness of the thoracic box it resists lateral pressure, so that in the middle of the wing stroke (Fig. 5.5 A(ii), B(ii)) the wing articulation is unstable and the wings, passing through this point, flick rapidly into the up or down position. This is known as a *click mechanism,* and the sudden changes in muscle tension which it produces are important in the operation of the wing muscles.

These simple statements conceal a wealth of variation in wing structure, wing-hinge form and function, the role of elasticity of the thorax and the adjustments of orientation of the wing during both upbeat and downbeat (which increase its efficiency as an aerofoil (Fig. 5.6) and allow some control of flight orientation).

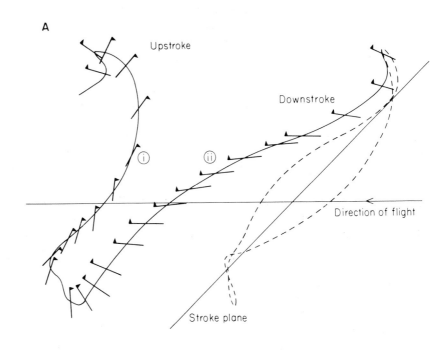

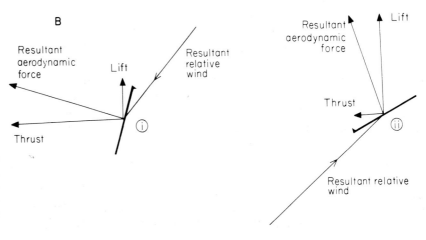

Fig. 5.6. Diagrams to illustrate the aerodynamics of the wing of an insect, such as a blowfly, during flight.
A, The closed loop (broken line) represents the path traced by the wing-tip relative to the insect, during one wingbeat cycle; the open loop (solid curve) shows the same path when the forward movement of the insect is taken into account. The short bars show the orientation of the wings at each point in the cycle, the small triangle indicating the morphological upper surface and leading edge. Note that the wing moves downwards and forwards, and upwards and backwards, and that during part of the upstroke, the wing is inverted.
B, The diagrams represent the forces acting on the wings at approximately the middle of the upstroke (i) and of the downstroke (ii) (cf. **A** above); the thick line represents the chord of the wing. The resultant relative wind is due to the movement both of the wing and of the insect. The resultant aerodynamic force experienced by the wing can be resolved into a horizontal component (thrust) and a vertical component (lift). Note that, due to the twisting of the wing and its backward movement, lift is developed even on the upstroke (After Nachtigall, W. (1974) *Insects in Flight.* George Allen & Unwin Ltd, London).

However, they form the background against which we may consider aspects of the physiology of nerves and muscles used in flight.

Synchronous flight muscles (§5.1) are found in members of the Odonata, Orthoptera and Lepidoptera, and asynchronous flight muscles (§5.1) occur in the Diptera, Hymenoptera, Coleoptera, Thysanoptera and most Hemiptera. It is in these latter insects with asynchronous muscles that the highest wingbeat frequencies are found. In the blowfly, *Calliphora,* a wingbeat frequency of about 120 Hz is driven by a motor nerve firing frequency of only 3 Hz. Moreover, no electrical activity can be detected in the contracting muscle membrane when the axons are not actually firing. Experiments show that the capacity for sustained rhythmic contraction and relaxation depends on the properties of the muscles and on the elasticity of the thorax.

If the muscle is soaked in glycerol (which removes all the cell contents except the myofibrils) and then supplied with Mg-ATP and Ca^{++}, the myofibrillar skeleton can still be made to contract rhythmically at about the natural wingbeat frequency. This happens if the muscle is suitably stretched and set into oscillation by a mechanical device. Stretching the fibrils results in a slightly delayed contraction, and release of tension promotes a similarly delayed relaxation. Thus, the muscle adds impetus to the already oscillating system and provides the energy to maintain the rhythmic movement. In the intact insect, the thoracic box and wings together act as a resonating system, and the duration and timing of muscle contraction are mechanically induced so as to keep the structure vibrating, and the insect flying. The activity is started by muscle contraction under direct nervous command, but after that the nervous input merely regulates the availability of Ca^{++} and hence the power output of the oscillating system.

The wings exert most power on the downstroke, but on the upstroke much of the power supplied by the muscles is used to distort the thorax, and particularly the highly elastic cuticular protein, *resilin* (p. 28), situated at the wing hinge. Most of the power thus stored is released on the downstroke, as the thorax resumes its original shape, and adds to the power actually being produced by the muscles at that time. Insects with synchronous flight muscles also utilize the elasticity of the thorax, but here individual wingbeats are driven by suitably oscillating motor nerve outputs, causing contractions in wing elevator muscles and wing depressors alternately. There are two small groups of reciprocally active motor neurones in both the meso- and metathoracic ganglia. These neurones are coupled by interneurones with excitatory or inhibitory synapses to keep them oscillating coherently. The motor neurones may generate their own flight rhythm or they may be driven by a common, appropriately coupled, interneuronal oscillator. This point is not yet resolved. Despite the built-in rhythmicity of this system there is still a considerable plasticity of wing action: different numbers of motor units may be recruited to vary the power output; the number of nerve impulses per contraction may vary, either bilaterally to adjust overall power output, or unilaterally to effect turning; turning may also be accomplished by unilateral frequency changes, or changes of phase between the two sides.

Thus, power output and steering may be controlled by modifying the output from the central neural programme to the 'flight motor', but in many insects, particularly in the more advanced ones, the muscles which control flight are separated from those which produce power. In *Calliphora,* for example, apart from the flight motor, there are 17 pairs of muscles which, by acting on the skeleton, control various parameters of wing movement, including frequency, amplitude and angle of attack.

These adjustments are, essentially, reflex responses (§6.1) and they vary greatly in their rate of operation. In locusts, amplitude and frequency are regulated by the output of a stretch receptor which fires towards the end of each upstroke. Many wingbeat cycles may elapse before the rhythmic output of the flight motor neurones is adjusted to the appropriate level. Campaniform sensilla (§4.5.1) at the wing base produce a much more rapid reflex adjustment of wing angle. Many such reflexes have been described and, although simple in themselves, appear to be part of more sophisticated and interdependent mechanisms for flight regulation.

5.3.2 Walking

The walking gait of most insects consists of alternating tripods of support in which the first and third legs on one side and the second leg on the other side are in contact with the substratum at any one time, and legs on opposite sides of each segment step alternately. This basic gait is subject to modification, particularly as the speed of walking varies, in which case phase drifts occur between the legs of each tripod. Because of unevenness in the substrate, the load on a given leg varies unpredictably so that sensory feedback is probably important in controlling each step. At higher stepping frequencies this effect may be less important and the control more dependent on a central programme.

Evidence for a central programme has been found in cockroaches (see also cricket singing, §6.1.5). With sensory input removed, alternating bursts of firing occur in motor neurones driving antagonistic walking muscles. The output from the central programme can be augmented by reflex sensory feedback, however. During retraction of a leg (the power stroke), campaniform sensilla (§4.5.1) at the base of the leg fire and supply a positive feedback to the central motor system, reinforcing its activity. The relative effectiveness of this peripheral feedback is decreased if the level of activity of the motor neurones is raised, suggesting that the central programme is of greatest importance in highly excited insects. Variable interaction between central mechanisms and peripheral feedback also appears to govern coordination of leg movements between segments (§4.7.4).

Evidence for this sort of interaction has been found at the individual muscle level in the metathoracic femur of the locust. It houses two antagonistic muscles, an extensor and a flexor, which move the more distal segment, the tibia. The tibial extensor is innervated by a fast and a slow axon (§5.1.2) and by a branch of an inhibitor neurone shared by other muscles as well. The slow and inhibitor axons fire during standing or walking, but the fast axon fires only during jumping or kicking. The activity of the slow axon is affected by feedback from receptors measuring muscle tension in the femur and from sensilla on the tarsus. The tarsal sensilla also affect the activity of the inhibitor. During fast walking, output from the slow axon to the extensor alternates with output from other neurones to its antagonist, the flexor. The inhibitor to the extensor fires briefly just before the flexor burst starts and is believed to accelerate relaxation of the extensor.

Further reading

Hoyle G. (1975) The neural control of skeletal muscles. In *Insect Muscle,* ed. P. N. R. Usherwood. Academic Press, London.

Hughes G. M. & Mill P. J. (1974) Locomotion: Terrestrial. In *The Physiology of Insecta.* Vol. 3 (2nd edn.), ed. M. Rockstein. Academic Press, New York.

Nachtigall W. (1974) *Insects in Flight.* George Allen and Unwin, London.

Pringle J. W. S. (1975) *Insect Flight.* Oxford Biology Readers 52. Oxford University Press.

Chapter 6
Behaviour

6.1 THE NEURAL BASIS OF BEHAVIOUR

6.1.1 Reflexes and responses

Behaviour is very much a part of physiology. Indeed, it is the most complex part, consisting as it does of the motor output of myriad integrated neural events. The physiological 'unit' of behaviour—so far as it can be thought of in that way—is the *response,* or *reflex*: a behavioural act elicited as a reaction to a stimulus. In insects this consists, at its simplest, of a segmental reflex, comparable to the vertebrate's spinal reflex arc. Thus, when a cockroach is tapped on one leg with the leg of another cockroach, it kicks back with the leg that was tapped. The terms response and reflex are roughly synonymous, but the latter is usually restricted to simpler motor patterns of the 'knee-jerk' type, whereas the former is generally used when more complex behaviours are involved.

All behavioural responses consist of three elements: (1) transduction of the stimulus by sense organ into an afferent electrical signal sent to the central nervous system (CNS) (§4.5); (2) integration of this signal with other relevant sensory inputs, by interneurones within the CNS (§4.7); (3) transmission of an efferent command to the motor system (muscles) to produce an overt behavioural act (§5.2). Responses occur in this way both as reactions to external stimuli from the environment and as reactions to internal stimuli from within the insect. In the latter case they may appear to occur spontaneously, as, for example, in 'spontaneous' activity due to circadian rhythms (§6.3, 7.4). To the observer, the insect's behaviour consists of only the last element of the response—the motor act—but the form that that takes is determined mainly by the second, central element, particularly in relation to the strength of the stimulus.

Responses probably never occur as fixed actions regardless of circumstance; they are modifiable if other inputs conflict with them. The old mechanistic concept of behaviour as being just a complex series of push-button, stimulus/response reflexes has long since been abandoned, even for apparently stereotyped behaviour of the 'knee-jerk' type. There is, rather, a continuum of response types, ranging from so-called '*fixed action patterns*', which tend to occur in an almost constant form regardless of stimulus strength (once that is above threshold), to highly labile responses whose level of performance is strongly stimulus-dependent. Adult eclosion is an extreme example of the first type, since once stimulated by a light-dark signal or by the insect's circadian clock (§7.4) it always occurs to completion. Blowfly feeding is an example of the other extreme, with the volume of sugar solution ingested being directly proportional to its concentration.

The behaviour of insects is to some extent organized segmentally; they can, for example, walk in a more or less co-ordinated fashion after they have been decapitated, and an isolated thoracic segment of a cockroach can even learn to prevent its leg receiving an electric shock. Thus the neuromuscular co-ordination of flight, walking, respiration, copulation, and eating is organized largely within and between the relevant segments (§5.3, 6.1.5). The brain's role lies mainly in integrating the competing reflexes in relation to the information coming in from the principal sense organs, and in relation to the insect's previous experience and its physiological state. Whether at the segmental or cerebral level, however, the integration—and *causation*—of behaviour depend on neurophysiological phenomena, particularly on latency, summation, after-discharge, fatigue, excitation and inhibition—terms first defined by C. S. Sherrington in his classical work on the spinal reflexes of decerebrate dogs. These terms in their modern usage, have been considered from the electrophysiological point of view in Chapter 4; we will here look at them at the behavioural level.

6.1.2   Latency and summation

When any animal is stimulated, there is always a small delay between the arrival of the stimulus at the sense organ and the appearance of a measurable motor response. This *latency* is due in part to the time taken for the sense cell to respond and for impulse conduction round the reflex arc, but is due mainly to the phenomenon of '*summation*', whereby more than one incoming spike must arrive at a synapse before the post-synaptic cell will generate an onward-going spike. Neurophysiologically, this normally therefore involves synaptic facilitation, as well as the more simple summation of pre-synaptic spikes (§4.7.2). Behaviourally, it can be seen in two forms: *temporal 'summation'*, in which maintenance or repetition of a stimulus at a single sensory site evokes a response that is not evoked by brief stimulation or by an isolated stimulus; and *spatial 'summation'*, in which stimuli applied simultaneously to different sensory sites evoke a response when stimulation of one site alone does not.

This provides a first level of behavioural control, by preventing responses to trivial stimuli, and by the latency being inversely proportional to the stimulus strength so that the stronger the stimulus, the quicker the response. Thus when a blowfly's tarsal chemo-receptors are touched with a drop of 0.2 M NaCl solution there is a delay of 100 ms before the fly retracts its proboscis, but when the solution is 0.5 M the delay is only 60 ms. This must be due to temporal summation, with the stronger solution generating more sensory spikes per unit time. Spatial summation can be seen in the response the fly makes to sucrose stimulation of the proboscis: the threshold concentration necessary to elicit proboscis extension is 0.42 M if only one sensory hair on the labellum is stimulated, 0.06 M if 2 hairs are stimulated together, 0.03 if 3 hairs are, and 0.01 if either 4 hairs or the whole labellum is stimulated. The biological significance is clear: a particle of food so small that it stimulates only one hair is not worth expending energy to eat unless its food value is high, whereas one that covers at least four hairs is, unless its food value is very low.

6.1.3   After-discharge and fatigue

Although most sensory cells cease to fire the instant their stimulation stops, it is characteristic of behaviour that the motor response continues on for some time afterwards, as what Sherrington called an *after-discharge*. Moreover, like latency, after-discharge is proportional to stimulus intensity, as can be seen in the 'dance' a hungry blowfly performs having chanced upon a small droplet of sugar solution and eaten it. Although stimulation of its external chemoreceptors thereupon ceases, for several seconds the fly performs repeated turns (a klinokinesis—Table 6.1, p. 95) and probings with its proboscis, as if it were 'looking for' another drop. The duration of this dance is proportional to the sugar concentration. A drop of 1.0 M may elicit a dance of 15-20 180° turns, a drop of 0.5 M perhaps 6 turns, and a drop of 0.1 M only about 3.

By contrast, whenever a stimulus is maintained for a while or is repeated at frequent intervals without 'reward', the response to it wanes even though the stimulation is still occurring. This Sherringtonian 'fatigue' (which is not to be confused with *muscle fatigue* due to biochemical exhaustion of the muscles) involves several levels of neuronal integration. Centrally, it involves interneuronal *habituation* (§4.7.2). Peripherally, it may also involve sensory *adaptation* (§4.3.2), though the response often wanes while the receptors continue to respond normally. House flies, for example, repeatedly visit any new object placed in their cage, and the number of visits they pay to it declines exponentially during the first 30 min. There is no reason to suppose, however, that their eyes provide the brain with information about the object that is in any way different at the beginning and end of this period (see §4.7.2).

6.1.4   Excitation and inhibition

Undoubtedly the most important central nervous phenomena in the integration of behaviour are *excitation* and *inhibition* (§4.3.2, 4.7), with the latter performing the less apparent but nevertheless probably dominant role (§4.7.4). The most obvious level at which this occurs is in the co-ordination of antagonistic and allied pairs of

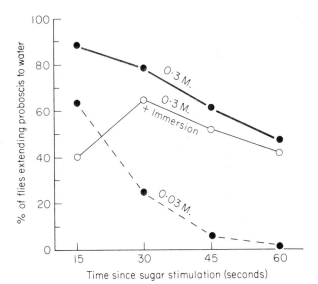

Fig. 6.1. Raised central excitability in blowflies (*Phormia regina*), shown by changes in the responsiveness of the proboscis extension reflex. The fly is first allowed to drink to satiation with water, after which it will not extend its proboscis when stimulated on the labellum with water. Sucrose solution is then briefly touched to the labellum (at time 0) and the fly tested with water again at intervals over the next 60 s. The effect of the sugar stimulation is to lower the threshold for water so that most flies now extend the proboscis to water stimulation. The level of this raised excitability is proportional to the stimulation intensity (cf. the 0.3 M and 0.03 M sucrose curves), and declines back to zero over a period of *c.* 100 s. Raised central inhibition is demonstrable in the same experiment: a 3-s immersion in water greatly depresses the excitability of the flies normally caused by stimulation with 0.3 M sucrose (cf. thin and thick solid lines) (After Dethier, V. G. (1976) *The Hungry Fly*. pp. 418-442. Harvard University Press, Cambridge, Mass.).

muscles in simple reflexes such as walking or flight (§5.3). Behaviour at all levels, however, is integrated by central excitation and inhibition in essentially the same way—the more complex the behaviour, the more of the CNS involved and the more complex the interactions. The landing response of a flying insect, for example, cannot be elicited without the flight motor first being inhibited; nor can the insect take off without first inhibiting its tarsal grip on the substrate. Perhaps less obviously, many responses occur more readily (i.e. their thresholds are lowered) because of the excitatory effect of preceding responses. For example, a water-satiated blowfly will not extend its proboscis when the labellum is stimulated with water, but will do so if it is given a brief stimulation with sugar just before the water stimulation (Fig. 6.1). The effect of the sugar stimulation is to create a heightened level of excitation in the CNS (known as a *central excitatory state*) so that the threshold for the response to water is lowered. Note that this increased responsiveness occurs centrally and is not due to peripheral changes (e.g. in receptor sensitivity—see §4.7.4). Furthermore, it is proportional to the intensity of the excitatory stimulus (sugar) and outlasts it, as an after-discharge, by many seconds.

Conversely, *central inhibitory states* also occur, though because they are essentially negative in effect they are less easy to demonstrate behaviourally. One form they may take can be shown in the blowfly, however, by using the same experiment and measuring the degree to which an 'unpleasant' stimulus reduces the central excitation created by sugar stimulation. Thus the strong stimulus of immersing the fly in water for 3 s, before stimulating it with sugar, greatly reduces its subsequent responsiveness to water (Fig. 6.1, thin line). The immersion in water apparently produces a central effect lasting for at least 15 s, which interferes, presumably by inhibition, with the generation of the longer-lasting excitation by sugar. It is important to realize that many responses involve central programmes (§4.7.4 and pp. 79-80); that are blocked by central inhibition for most of the time. (When this inhibition is switched off (*disinhibition*), the response then occurs apparently 'spontaneously'. Thus when the female *Mantis* eats the head off her male partner, his copulating reflexes, previously held in inhibition by the sub-oesophageal ganglion, are dis-inhibited and occur without external stimulation (though presumably internal, proprioceptive feedback is still necessary).

One important manifestation of excitation is *post-inhibitory rebound*. This occurs after one of a pair of competing responses has been inhibited for a while by the performance of the other. When the first response ceases, the competing response, now released from inhibition, reappears with increased vigour. For example, the rate of climb of a flying aphid is markedly increased by a brief landing on a leaf (Fig. 6.2A), and the speed of walking by a locust is momentarily raised by a brief rest (Fig. 6.2B). In a sense, this is the converse of habituation, in which prolonged excitation of a

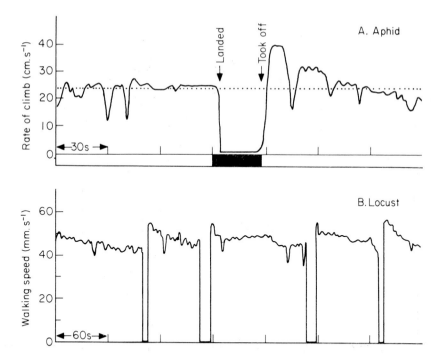

Fig. 6.2. Post-inhibitory 'rebound' demonstrated in flying aphids (*Aphis fabae*) and walking locust nymphs (*Locusta migratoria*). **A**, The aphid is climbing at a steady rate of *c.* 24 mm.s⁻¹ when it is offered a leaf on which to land; this it promptly does, but soon takes off again, whereupon the leaf is immediately removed from view. The response to this 25-s inhibition of flight is a greatly raised rate of climb lasting for several seconds. Black bar shows period when leaf was in view; dotted line, average rate of climb before leaf presented (After Kennedy, J. S. (1965) *J. exp. Biol.* **43**, 489-509). **B**, A similar rebound phenomenon is shown after four spontaneous pauses in walking by a locust; each 5-10-s inhibition of walking induces a brief acceleration, from the normal steady 45 mm.s⁻¹ to *c.* 55 mm.s⁻¹ (After Moorhouse, J. E. *et al.* (1978) *J. exp. Biol.* **72**, 1-16).

response leads to a period when it becomes relatively inexcitable. These two interactions—post-inhibitory rebound and post-excitatory refractoriness—are important components in the balanced integration of all animal behaviour.

6.1.5 The integration of cricket singing—a model example

All these neural phenomena, intervening between the receipt of a stimulus and the output of a motor command, determine how a response occurs. Multiplexed in time and interacting at many levels in the CNS, they are the components out of which behaviour is built. Just how this creates the infinite subtleties of complex behaviour is probably better understood in crickets than in any other animal—thanks primarily to the work of F. Huber and his colleagues.

Male crickets (*Gryllus campestris*) produce three types of song (Fig. 6.3 A-C): 'calling', 'courtship' and 'rivalry'. The songs are produced by the rubbing of a file on one forewing over a ridge on the other, and appear to the human ear as a series of 'chirps', each syllable in the chirp being produced by one inward movement of the

wings. Calling songs attract receptive females by evoking a positive phonotaxis in them (Table 6.1 p. 95); courtship songs are performed in close proximity to a female, stimulating her to mount the male; rivalry songs are produced during strong antennal contact with another male (or an unreceptive female) and evoke either fighting or fleeing. The songs are perceived via tympanal organs ('ears') in the tibia of each fore-leg. The great value of this behaviour to the neurobiologist is that the song patterns are highly structured and can be recognized electrophysiologically in both the singer and the hearer, not only peripherally in their muscles or auditory organs, but also deep within the CNS.

As with walking and flight (§5.3, 6.1.1), the neuromuscular co-ordination of a song is a segmental reflex, with the muscles that move the forewings being innervated mainly from the mesothoracic ganglion. A central neural programme exists in this ganglion, which can organize a complete song when suitably stimulated via descending nerve fibres in the neck ventral nerve cord. The song pattern is due to neural oscillators (p. 79) which regulate both the syllable interval within the chirp (at *c.* 40 Hz) and the interval between chirps (at *c.* 3 Hz). These oscillatory circuits can, moreover,

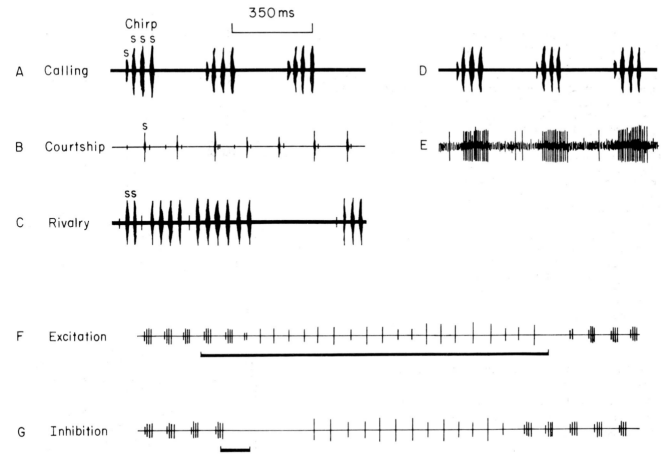

Fig. 6.3. Neural control of cricket (*Gryllus campestris*) singing behaviour. **A, B** and **C,** Oscilloscope records of the three song types; each vertical mark is one 'syllable' (s) caused by one wing movement (see text); height of marks is proportional to sound intensity; calling chirp rate is about 3 Hz (time scale above). **D,** Calling song evoked by stimulating the brain (at 80 Hz). **E,** Action potentials recorded from an interneurone in the neck connective during play-back of a recorded calling song that was timed as in trace **D**; this cell evidently codes for chirp duration, with a slight latency of *c.* 5 ms. **F,** Switch up from spontaneous calling to courtship singing evoked by excitatory (depolarizing) 80-Hz stimulation of the brain, timed as shown by bar under trace; note return to calling at end of excitation. **G,** Switching off of spontaneous calling by inhibitory (hyperpolarizing) stimulation of the brain, at bar under trace; note post-inhibitory rebound to courtship singing *c.* 0.5 s after end of inhibition, followed by return to calling (After Huber, F. (1974) in *The Biology of Brains,* ed. Broughton, W. B., Institute of Biology, London, pp. 61-88).

organize the song without the aid of peripheral sensory feedback, since the firing pattern in the nerves to the wing opener and closer muscles is unchanged when all the peripheral nerves in the thorax are cut, when the forewings are removed or loaded with weights, or even when the muscles themselves are cut through.

Which of the three songs is produced, however, depends on input from the brain. Electrically stimulating the cut ends of the nerve cord in a beheaded male at different frequencies produces different songs (e.g. 17 Hz evokes calling; 57 Hz evokes courtship), as also will similar stimulation in the brain of intact males (Fig. 6.3 D). This is not due to any direct coupling with the stimulus oscillation, however, since a change in that from 2 to 80 Hz produces only a 17% increase in chirp frequency.

Normally, of course, switches between songs occur, *inter alia,* in response to auditory input from other crickets. Initial interpretation of songs is performed by the auditory nerves, whose neurones act as a frequency filter by having their peak sensitivity at the energy peaks emitted in their own species' song. Their input to the prothoracic ganglion is then encoded (§4.5.3) by inter-neurones whose output to the brain can be monitored in the nerve cord connectives in the neck. Some neurones code for chirp duration (Fig. 6.3 E), others for syllable frequency, and so on. The heard song thus passes to the brain as a series of coded signals which must then be integrated with other inputs and result in the issuing of the appropriate motor command back to the meso-thoracic ganglion.

Since electrical stimulation of many sites within the brain evokes songs and, indeed, locomotion too (which, of course, is also involved in courtship and rivalry behaviour), the integration must involve widespread neural interactions and be highly complex. Although some of the relevant neuropile areas in the brain have been localized, very little is yet known of their neural 'wiring'. This contrasts with what is known about the thoracic co-ordination of the song patterns, for which many of the oscillatory and reciprocally inhibitory antagonistic neurones have been identified. On the other hand, however complex the brain's neural interactions may be, it is clear that they involve relatively well-understood synaptic phenomena.

Behavioural observation suggests that the three song types are arranged in a hierarchy of ascending levels of arousal: calling < courtship < rivalry. It is therefore interesting that crickets implanted with microelectrodes in the brain, but free to walk (in which state they live for weeks), can have their song type controlled by electrical stimulation. Thus if brief excitatory (i.e. depolarizing—§4.3.2) stimulation is used, a calling chirp can be evoked and a calling song gradually built up by successive increases in stimulus duration, until the excitation becomes sustained as a long-lasting after-discharge, and the song free runs without further stimulation. Similarly, when a male is calling spontaneously, it can be switched up to a courtship song by such excitation (Fig. 6.3 F), and switched up again to a rivalry song by still stronger excitation. Conversely, spontaneous songs can be stopped by inhibitory (i.e. hyperpolarizing) stimulation (Fig. 6.3.G). Furthermore, post-inhibitory rebound (§6.1.4) occurs after such

inhibition, since after calling has been inhibited, court-ship may be the first song to reappear when the inhibition stops (Fig. 6.3 G). Evidently, what to sing and whether to sing or not is determined in the cricket's brain largely by the balance between excitation and inhibition in relation to stimulus intensity.

The overall organization and control of cricket singing thus exhibits in a nutshell all the neural phenomena that behaviour is assumed to consist of: a sensory system with pattern-specific afferent coding; central motor programmes involving neural oscillators; long-lasting after-discharge in central excitatory (and presumably inhibitory) states; and balanced excitatory/inhibitory integration including rebound. Whereas this should de-mystify some of the physiological basis of insect behaviour, it should by no means be thought that the surface of the problem has been more than scratched—for one thing, no other kind of insect has been examined in anything approaching this detail.

6.2 CHANGING RESPONSIVENESS—OR 'DRIVE' AND 'MOTIVATION'

The phenomena considered in §6.1 primarily concern the organization of insect behaviour on a time-scale of seconds or minutes. However, behaviour also changes over the much longer time-scales of hours, days and life-times, under the influence of factors such as 'drive', circadian rhythms (§6.3), sexual maturation (§6.4), and learning (§6.5).

Animals do not always respond in the same way when offered the same stimulus. A blowfly that has fed recently will not extend its proboscis when stimulated with 0.1 M sucrose, but will do so a few hours later. Similarly, a fly that is water-satiated will not extend its proboscis to water, but will do so after being prevented from drinking for a while. Colloquially, we call these food-deprived and water-deprived states of heightened responsiveness 'hunger' and 'thirst'. Scientifically, the terms *drive* or *motivation* are usually used, in an attempt to avoid such anthropomorphic concepts. The hungry fly is said to have a high 'feeding drive' or to be strongly 'motivated to feed'. There is a danger in using these terms blindly, however, because it implies that the phrases 'feeding drive' or 'feeding motivation' are more objective than the word 'hunger', whereas their use is in

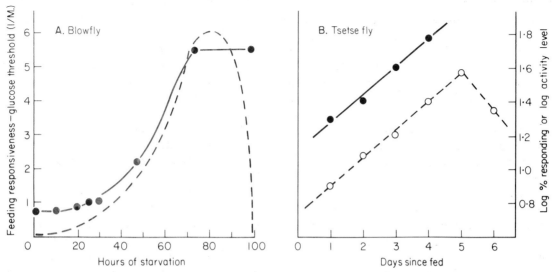

Fig. 6.4. Changing responsiveness in blowflies (*Phormia regina*) and tsetse flies (*Glossina morsitans*) due to 'hunger'. In both figures the flies were fed to repletion at time 0 (the blowfly on sugar water, the tsetse on blood), and the dotted curves show the changing levels of spontaneous flight activity (in arbitrary units); shortly before death activity level declines rapidly in both species. The solid lines show changing responsiveness to food-associated stimuli: in **A** as the threshold concentration of glucose necessary to elicit proboscis extension (expressed as the reciprocal of the molarity), and in **B** as the (log) percentage of flies responding to a slowly moving vertical black stripe (simulated host movement) by taking off and flying towards it. Note that the behavioural change is exponential: **A** is plotted on a linear scale, but **B** on a logarithmic one (**A**, After Green, G. W. (1964) *J. Insect Physiol.* **10**, 711-726, and Evans, D. R. & Dethier, V. G. (1957) *J. Insect Physiol.* **1**, 3-17; **B**, after Brady, J. (1975) *J. Insect Physiol.* **21**, 807-829).

effect teleological, describing the behaviour, not in terms of its mechanism, but in terms of its end result—feeding. Drive and motivation are often used as convenient shorthand to identify such changing levels of responsiveness in relation to specific physiological conditions (starvation, water-deprivation, raised sex hormone levels, etc.), but it must always be borne in mind that their use does not mean that anything about the behaviour so-labelled has thereby been explained.

'Hunger' and 'thirst' are particularly clear examples of this difficulty. Some insects, especially sedentary phytophagous species such as aphids, feed almost continuously. Most, however, feed intermittently and invariably become more responsive to food stimuli the longer it is since they last fed. Typically this relationship is exponential, both in frequent feeders like the blowfly, and in infrequent ones like the blood-sucking tsetse fly (Fig. 6.4, solid lines). What happens is that the threshold for the relevant stimulus falls progressively (i.e. responsiveness increases) in relation to the physiological need

for food. In addition, however, starvation not only increases responsiveness to specific, food-associated stimuli, but also increases spontaneous activity (Fig. 6.4, broken lines), and the level of other responses too. Hunger is in fact a complex behavioural phenomenon involving the central modulation of many responses. In species which drink as a separate behaviour from feeding, the same kind of changes in responsiveness to water are involved in 'thirst' developed during water-deprivation.

6.3   CIRCADIAN RHYTHMS IN BEHAVIOUR

Perhaps the greatest single influence that changes insect behaviour is their daily, circadian rhythm (§7.4); a given species is always nocturnal, diurnal, or crepuscular, and will not normally be found moving about at other times. Experimentally, this is usually demonstrated by measuring so-called 'spontaneous' locomotor activity, that is, running, walking, or flight occurring in the absence of

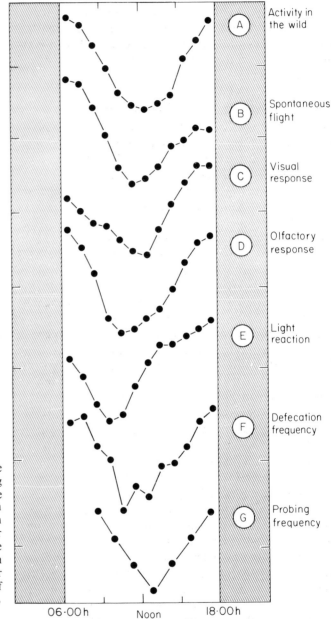

Fig. 6.5. Daily (circadian) changes in various behaviours of the tsetse fly (*Glossina morsitans*). **A**, The number of flies coming to feed in the wild on a bait ox in Africa. **B, C** and **D**, The percentage of flies taking off each hour: **B**, spontaneously in actographs; **C**, to a moving stripe (see Fig. 6.3**B**); **D**, to human odour. **E**, The proportion of flies resting on brighter rather than darker surfaces. **F**, The frequency of defecation. **G**, The proportion of flies probing a warm sponge. All are shown on arbitary ordinate scales against the 12 daylight hours in order to demonstrate the close similarity between the patterns of changing responsiveness (After Brady, J. (1975) *J. Ent. (A),* **50**, 79-95).

any changing stimuli from the environment (see Fig. 7.2). However, the circadian rhythm has a much more profound effect on behaviour than this might imply, for it is not only 'spontaneous' activity that changes across the day, but also the thresholds of a whole battery of other responses. Thus, in the tsetse fly, 'spontaneous' flight goes through a daily V-shaped rhythm with peaks in the morning and evening, but the responsiveness to stimuli such as host movement, odour, feeding surfaces, and resting sites also varies in almost exactly the same manner (Fig. 6.5). It appears that much of the fly's behaviour is coupled to the clock that controls its circadian rhythm, so that the thresholds of many responses are raised and lowered together across the 24 hours. Less detailed experiments on other insects and on birds (and man) indicate that this is a quite general phenomenon.

6.4 HORMONES AND BEHAVIOUR

Behaviour can be changed more or less instantaneously by electrophysiological phenomena (§6.1), relatively permanently by neural growth during development (and perhaps during learning—§6.5), or, between these two time-scales, by hormones. Apart from serving this medium-term function, hormones also have the advantage that just a few endocrine cells can be used to communicate with virtually every cell in the nervous system—via the blood stream. Insects have exploited this possibility extensively, presumably because it is an economic way to regulate behaviour for a small animal with a limited volume of nervous tissue. The main disadvantage is that the regulation is inevitably less sensitive and less easy to turn on and off than is direct neural control.

Hormones cause marked changes in insect behaviour in three different ways. First, they influence the growth of neurones so that at metamorphosis, for example, larval behaviour is switched off and adult behaviour switched on. Second, they affect the growth of other tissues which may change the associated sensory input and hence the relevant responses (e.g. juvenile hormone (JH) stimulating egg-development, which releases oviposition behaviour). Third, they act directly on nerves to change both spontaneous neural activity (§4.8.3) and behavioural responsiveness, apparently by altering central thresholds (presumably by facilitating or inhibiting synapses). In this last, they may act either as *releasers* (e.g. as in eclosion hormone, the circadian-controlled secretion of which releases emergence behaviour in silkmoth pupae—§4.8.3, 7.4), or as *modifiers* (e.g. JH altering sexual responsiveness in male locusts); the difference is probably only of degree, however.

It is sexual behaviour that has been most extensively studied—in relation to how it is affected by hormones from the brain, corpora allata, or corpora cardiaca (§3.3.1), and by feedback from tissues such as the ovary and spermathecae. For example, if the corpora allata (and hence JH) are removed from young virgin *Gomphocerus* grasshoppers or *Leucophaea* cockroaches, they fail to develop receptivity to males, whom they kick away. But when corpora allata are implanted back into such refractory, allatectomized females, they become sexually receptive. That this behavioural change is due to a hormone can be further demonstrated by applying synthetic JH to the allatectomized females, which has the same effect. Furthermore, JH not only switches on sexual receptivity in virgins, but also maintains it in mature females, who revert to being refractory within a few days of being allatectomized.

JH is not the only hormone concerned in this change of responsiveness, however, since if the brain neurosecretory cells are extirpated from allatectomized females, corpora allata implantation does not restore their sexual receptivity. There is also a suggestion of an ovarial influence, since castrated *Chorthippus* (grasshopper) females lose their receptivity, which can then be partly restored by a blood transfusion from normal females. In moths (*Antheraea* and *Hyalophora*), though apparently not in grasshoppers or cockroaches, a hormone from the corpora cardiaca is also involved, in this case in evoking sex-pheromone release in virgin females (§6.6). The roles and relative importance of the different hormones involved vary more widely between species than these few examples suggest. However, it seems likely that the varied experimental results reported are often due to the existence of small species-specific differences in critical effective hormone titres (cf. JH and migration—§7.3).

Non-sexual behaviour has been much less studied, but is likewise affected by hormones. Thus, corpus cardiacum secretions and JH are probably involved in regulating locomotor activity levels, ecdysone may be involved in locust aggregation behaviour, JH is involved in migration (§7.3), and eclosion hormone is certainly involved in releasing emergence movements in pupal moths (§7.4). The fact that insects have employed mainly morphogenetic hormones (i.e. JH, etc.) to control their behaviour is intriguing. It seems to imply the co-evolution of behavioural changes with the complexity of development, and the need to link the two.

6.5 LEARNING

Learning is relatively long-lasting modification of behaviour as a result of experience. It may last for life, or only for a few hours or minutes. At its simplest in insects (as in all other animals), it consists of *habituation,* which is the loss of a response when a stimulus is repeated without reinforcement or 'reward' (§4.7.2, 6.1.2). At its most developed, it consists of complex operant conditioning. With their restricted nervous tissue and short life cycles, insects seem to have been subjected to little selective pressure to develop conditioned reflexes, so that much of their behaviour is in the form of genetically pre-determined, apparently stereotyped, instinctive responses. None of these instincts is really rigid, however (§6.1.1), and much of insect behaviour is modifiable by learning.

6.5.1 The conditioned reflex

A reflex is 'conditioned' when its motor act, which normally occurs in response to one form of stimulus, becomes associated with a new and different stimulus, and then occurs in response to that. In the classical conditioned reflex of Pavlov, the dog salivates reflexly (the unconditioned reflex—or UCR) to the stimulation of food in its mouth (the unconditioned stimulus—or UCS—the 'reward'), but if a bell is rung (as the conditioning stimulus—CS) just before or while the food is given, the dog's CNS associates the bell with food stimulation and, after a few trials, salivation occurs in response to the sound of the bell alone (the conditioned reflex—CR).

Classical conditioning, as this is called, is readily demonstrable in honey-bees. A bee fixed into a small tube so that it can scarcely move its head, will extend its proboscis (the UCR) when sugar water (the UCS) is touched to its antenna. If an odour (the CS) is presented to the antennae at the same time, after just a single training trial 80% of bees will subsequently extend the proboscis when the odour is given alone (the CR). The proboscis extension reflex can also be conditioned to a coloured light instead of an odour, but this is much harder for bees to learn and takes 50 or more paired (UCS + CS) trials before the 80% CR level is reached. Bees have to find scented and coloured flowers for food, so the value of this learning ability is obvious.

It also occurs, however, in other groups, including the Diptera. For example, in blowflies the proboscis extension reflex to sugar stimulation of the labellum (see p. 80) can be conditioned both to odours and to coloured lights, though not so readily as in bees. Note that the 'reward' may also be negative (i.e. 'unpleasant') so that the conditioned response then involves avoidance.

6.5.2 'Trial and error', or operant conditioning

In contrast to classical conditioning (§6.5.1), much of learning occurs in the absence of any obvious initial response, and is due instead to 'trial and error' learning, or *operant conditioning* as it is usually called. In insects, this commonly occurs as follows: (a) some piece of behaviour (e.g. flight) is initially performed without any obvious external stimulation (obvious to the observer, that is); (b) by chance this leads to the insect receiving a 'reward' (e.g. food); (c) a long-lasting connection is then made in the CNS between the behaviour (now a CR) and some other stimulus (now in effect a CS) to which the behaviour was previously only an unconditioned response. Thus a foraging honey-bee flies around its hive testing flowers until it finds one that is rich in nectar. This reward is then associated with various CS provided by the environment (colour and scent from the flower, direction from the sun), and the foraging behaviour is now conditioned to occur in response to these. The distinction between the two forms of learning, classical and operant, is not always very clear in practice. Consider a *Philanthus* wasp learning to recognize her nest site: does she learn the landmarks round the hole by classical or by operant conditioning?

6.5.3 Extinction, or 'forgetting'

If the habituated insect remained unresponsive for an indefinite period after the unrewarded stimulation ceased, it might then fail to respond to that stimulation when it next occurred significantly. Similarly, if a foraging bee continued to visit a patch of flowers after their nectar was exhausted, it would ultimately starve. 'Un-learning' is therefore as important as learning. For habituation this is called *dishabituation,* and occurs either when there is a change of some kind in the stimulus (§4.7.2), or when the unrewarded stimulus ceases, whereupon the response (as revealed by experimental test stimuli) gradually returns, usually over a period of a few minutes. For conditioned reflexes, this un-learning is called *extinction,* and occurs when the conditioned response is elicited repeatedly by the CS without reward. Occasionally a conditioned reflex is imprinted for life, as in the learning of host odours by larval parasitoids which, when adult, oviposit preferentially in surfaces with the same 'smell'. More usually, extinction occurs after a variable number of unrewarded responses, the number depending on such factors as the rapidity and frequency with which the CR was initially established.

6.6 PHEROMONES

Pheromones are species-specific chemical messengers. They may be single compounds or mixtures of compounds, and when released to the exterior by one animal cause particular reactions in others of the same species. They act in two ways: as *releasers,* when their effect is to evoke an immediate behavioural response; or as *primers,* when they stimulate or inhibit some physiological function such as gonad development (§6.7.2, 6.7.3). They are usually transmitted in the vapour phase as air-borne odours, but some are transferred to the recipient directly, and are then called *surface* or *contact pheromones.* Insects have developed this communication system to a uniquely high level of sophistication and importance, so that pheromones are involved in many aspects of their life: as sex 'attractants' (e.g. in moths and beetles), as 'alarm' signals (e.g. in aphids and ants), as copulation signals (e.g. in flies and bees), as aggregation signals (e.g. in cockroaches), as dispersal signals (e.g. in caterpillars), as gonad inhibition signals (e.g. in bees), as maturation signals (e.g. in locusts and termites), and so on.

Although it is in social species that pheromonal communication is developed to its greatest complexity (§6.7), the sensory physiology and behavioural mechanisms involved in the responses have been most closely studied in moths. There are two main reasons for this. First, the males are phenomenally sensitive to the female's scent (male *Bombyx* silkmoths respond to as little as 40 molecules s^{-1} of the pheromone 'bombykol') so their antennae provide an excellent model system for the study of chemoreceptor function (§4.5.1). Second, many moths are crop pests and may prove to be susceptible to control by behavioural manipulation with sex pheromones, many of which have been synthesized artificially. The sex pheromones of most species are mixtures of a few related compounds (commonly, straight-chain alcohols, acetates or ketones in the C_{10} to C_{16} range with a single double bond somewhere in the chain), and it is the *relative* concentrations of these that provides the species-specificity of the signal. Moreover, while the pheromone released by a 'calling' female elicits approach responses in conspecific males, it may actually inhibit such behaviour in males of closely related species.

How male moths are 'attracted' to calling females is described in §6.8.1; the role of primer pheromones in caste determination in social insects in §6.7.2 and §6.7.3; and the role of releaser pheromones in organizing social behaviour in §6.7.4.

6.7. SOCIAL BEHAVIOUR

6.7.1 Types of social behaviour

No other animals (except perhaps man) have evolved such complex sociality as the insects. Pre-social behaviour occurs throughout the class, in such activities as mating swarms in Ephemeroptera and Diptera, protective aggregations in web-spinning caterpillars and hibernating ladybirds, and parental care in earwigs and many bugs. But 'true', or *eusocial* behaviour (i.e. with co-operative brood care, overlap between generations, and a caste system) occurs only in the higher Hymenoptera and all Isoptera (termites). Although it has evidently evolved independently several times in the Hymenoptera, a common route seems to have been via parental care—first of the nest-provisioning, solitary wasp kind, then with the mother directly feeding the larvae, and finally with the first brood of daughters remaining virgin and helping the mother (the 'queen') to feed subsequent broods. Castes in the Hymenoptera are thus sex-specific, and sex is determined by whether the eggs are fertilized (female, diploid) or unfertilized (male, haploid). In the termites, by contrast, all castes occur equally in both sexes.

The key to eusocial organization is communication—via air-borne pheromones, trail pheromones (§6.7.4), mutual grooming (which transmits contact pheromones—

§6.6), and *trophallaxis* (the passage of liquid food from one individual to another). The communicating efficiency of this trophallaxis is remarkable: when 6 worker honey-bees were allowed to collect 20 ml of ^{32}P-labelled sucrose solution for 3 h, 29% of the 25 000 bees in the colony contained the label within 4 h, and 58% within 28 h. Such communication ensures that the colony is permeated with nest-specific odours so that intruders can be recognized and repelled; it also ensures that each member of the colony is dosed continually with the necessary caste-controlling primer pheromones (§6.7.2 and 6.7.3). The role of *hormones* in caste differentiation is considered in §3.3.6.

6.7.2   Caste system in honey-bees

The control of the caste structure in a honey-bee colony is maintained largely by a contact pheromone (§6.6) secreted from the queen's mandibular glands. This secretion, called '*queen substance*' (mainly 9-oxodecanoic acid) is licked off the queen by her attendants and then passed on to the other workers by trophallaxis (above). As long as it is maintained at a high concentration among the workers it inhibits the development of their ovaries (a primer effect—§6.6) and stops them from building the extra-large brood cells in which new, rival queens are reared (a releaser effect—§6.6).

This spread of queen substance through the colony evidently needs to be rapid and continuous, because workers become 'restless' within 30 min of the queen being removed, start building queen cells within a few hours, and start developing their ovaries within a few days. The same responses also occur when the concentration of queen substance falls for natural reasons, as when the queen becomes old, or the colony too large. The only means of reproduction and dispersal in honey-bees is by a new queen leaving the nest with a few thousand workers, as a 'swarm'. The effect of colony regulation by queen substance is thus three-fold: it stimulates the replacement of sick queens; it prevents premature swarming from debilitating small but otherwise healthy colonies; and it encourages swarming in large colonies that can afford the loss of workers.

6.7.3   Caste system in termites

The caste structure in termites is much more complicated than in any bees, but nevertheless appears to be regulated in a similar way by primer pheromones transmitted through the colony by trophallaxis. None of the pheromones involved have yet been identified chemically, but something of colony organization is understood in a few species—perhaps best in the primitive and relatively simple *Kalotermes flavicollis*. In this species, the colony is composed of a single pair of *primary reproductives* (the 'king' and 'queen'), various numbers of *larvae, nymphs, presoldiers* and *soldiers,* and a large number of *pseudergates.* All castes occur as both males and females and the developmental relationships between them are shown in Fig. 6.6.

As in all termites, a *Kalotermes* colony is founded by its king and queen after their mating flight from another colony. Normally they are the only fertile castes, but if either of them dies, nymphs, pseudergates and mature larvae of the relevant sex moult to become replacement reproductives, the excess being eaten by the pseudergates so that only a single royal pair survive. The same developmental response occurs if a group of pseudergates is isolated from the main colony. Alternatively, if there is a shortage of soldiers, the same stages may turn into soldiers, via an intermediary moult as a pre-soldier; and, again, excess soldiers are eaten by the pseudergates. The pseudergates are the main worker caste and either remain as such by repeated, non-differentiating (stationary) moults, or, in large colonies in spring, moult through to become winged adults which, after a mating flight in late summer will form a new colony elsewhere. In more advanced termite families, the caste system is both more complex than this and less labile as to developmental direction.

Few of these developmental switches in *Kalotermes* have been examined experimentally, but something is known of the pheromonal regulation by the king and queen of the differentiation of pseudergates into replacement reproductives (Fig. 6.6). At least seven pheromones seem to be involved, some being transmitted by proctodeal feeding—i.e. via anal/oral trophallaxis—and some in the vapour phase. The queen produces three pheromones; these stimulate the king to produce his pheromones, inhibit female pseudergates from developing into replacement reproductives, and stimulate the killing of surplus female replacement reproductives. The king produces the equivalent pheromones to control male pseudergates, and in addition a pheromone which

Fig. 6.6. The caste system and possible developmental routes in *Kalotermes flavicollis*. The *c.* 8 larval stages terminate in the development of a 'pseudergate'. This fully grown larva may undergo a number of 'stationary' moults and remain as a pseudergate more or less indefinitely; it may moult into a nymph (with wing buds) and then subsequently into a winged adult; it may moult and differentiate into a soldier; or it may develop directly into a replacement reproductive (this form is intermediate between a larva and an adult that has shed its wings). Any of the nymphs or late larval stages may produce soldiers or replacement reproductives, and nymphs may undergo 'regressive' moults to produce more pseudergates if required (After Lüscher, M. (1961) *Symp. R. ent. Soc. Lond.* **1**, 57-67).

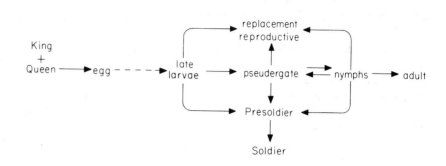

enhances the production of female replacement reproductives. Interestingly, whereas female pseudergates pass on the king's pheromone in the usual trophallactic way, they absorb the queen's pheromone that inhibits their own development and do not pass it on. The same trophallactic differentiation is true for male pseudergates: they absorb the king's male inhibitory pheromone but pass on the queen's pheromone (see also §3.3.6).

6.7.4 Pheromonal control of social behaviour

Pheromones are not only important as primers (§6.6) in controlling colony structure in social insects (§6.7.2, 6.7.3), they are also vital as releasers, in the organization of virtually every aspect of social behaviour. The signals may be single chemicals, with the response evoked being dependent on the context in which the signal is received—as in honey-bee queen substance acting to stop queen cell construction within the hive, attracting workers to a swarm outside the hive, or attracting males on the queen's nuptual flight. Alternatively, they may be mixtures of chemicals, with different relative concentrations of the components evoking different responses—as occurs with the defensive secretions of ants (cf. pheromonal species differentiation—§6.6). In this case, the different effects arise not so much because the defending ant secretes different proportions of the components (though that does occur), but because some components are more volatile than others, and

each therefore produces different areas of influence around the point of release (i.e. areas where their concentrations are above threshold for detection by other ants). These areas of influence are often called *active space*—see Fig. 6.7.

Herein lies a key to much of the apparent complex subtlety of higher social behaviour: pheromonal communication in a language of chemical component, concentration, and context. It is by this language that social insects manage their enormous co-operative feats: pulling large leaves together to weave nests, building huge earthen structures as termitaria, killing and carrying off relatively vast prey, etc. An example will illustrate the kind of mechanisms involved.

Many ants, such as the American fire ant, *Solenopsis*, lay pheromone-marked trails radiating out from their nests. Movement along these trails though appearing haphazard is in fact not so: the busier the trail, the more important the food source it leads to. But how do the ants inside the nest know which is the best food source? The answer lies in the statistical outcome of three effects. (1) An ant returning from a food source smears droplets of pheromone onto the ground from the tip of its sting, with a frequency that is directly proportional to the success it had in feeding. (2) The pheromone is highly volatile so that the droplets evaporate away quickly (in *c.* 2 min on glass). (3) Ants leave the nest to forage in numbers proportional to the concentration of

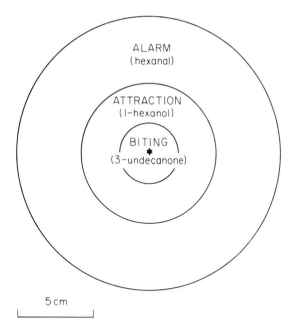

ALARM
(hexanal)

ATTRACTION
(1-hexanol)

BITING
(3-undecanone)

5 cm

Fig. 6.7. The different areas of '*active space*' surrounding the point of release of 'alarm' pheromone 20 s after its secretion by one *Oecophylla longinoda* worker ant (at point starred). The three named components of the pheromone each evoke different behavioural responses from other workers of the same species, but do so over different areas because their differential volatilities diffuse them (at above threshold concentration) over different distances from the point of release. '*Alarm*' involves increased random locomotor activity (i.e. klino- plus orthokinesis—Table 6.1); '*Attraction*' involves positive chemotaxis up the pheromone gradient to the release point; '*Biting*' involves attacking with the mandibles any available object (After Bradshaw, J. W. S. *et al.* (1979) *Physiol. Ent.* **4**, 15-25).

trail pheromone outside the nest, and so favour the more strongly marked trails. The resultant of these three forces is first an exponential build-up of workers along a trail to a new food source, then a levelling off as some workers begin to return from it without marking the trail because the food was so crowded that they had to leave it 'empty-handed', and finally a decline in the trail's use as the food becomes exhausted and better sources are found elsewhere. The overall effect is a dynamic balance in favour of optimal exploitation of food resources in relation to their size, richness, and nearness to the nest. By the same kind of stochastic process new nest sites are selected, ants moving hectically to and fro between potential sites, but gradually concen-

trating on the best one because it gets the most pheromone 'votes'.

With the striking exception of the honey-bee 'dance-language', it seems probable that much of the complex co-operative behaviour of social insects is explicable in similar terms, i.e. as the stochastic outcome of repertoires of responses to pheromonal 'language'. The long-enduring concept that colonies of eusocial insects are '*superorganisms*', with their individuals somehow analogous to the cells of a metazoan body, seems quite unnecessarily mystical.

6.8   ORIENTATION BEHAVIOUR

Much of any active animal's behaviour is taken up with orientational manoeuvres that serve to bring it to, get it away from, or keep it at particular sources of stimulation—e.g. food, mate, oviposition site, predator, high temperatures, dark areas, etc. Although such manoeuvres are sometimes highly complex (as in honey-bees navigating several kilometres by sun-compass to a patch of flowers), some of the responses involved are among the simplest of all behaviours (as in *Tenebrio* beetles ceasing to walk when the humidity is low). The various categories of these responses are summarized in Table 6.1.

6.8.1   Navigation to odour sources

When a walking insect is searching for the source of an odour (e.g. food), the olfactory stimuli may be present in sufficiently steep gradients on the ground or in the air to permit the insect to steer towards the source by *chemo-(tropo-) taxis* (Table 6.1). And if the odour is wind-borne, the insect merely needs to head upwind—steering by positive *anemotaxis*, i.e. by keeping its air movement detectors stimulated symmetrically on both sides of its body. In flight, however, orientation by this means is impossible because the insect is not in contact with the ground and therefore has no way of telling which way it is heading relative to the wind (cf. a man swimming in a river with his eyes shut).

This problem arises in two common situations: in pheromonally-stimulated mate finding, and in host odour-stimulated food or oviposition-site finding. In both cases the same orientational strategy is used: optomotor-guided positive anemotaxis (Table 6.1).

Table 6.1 ORIENTATION BEHAVIOUR—CLASSIFICATION

I. Kineses—responses to *non-directional* stimuli (*e.g.* ambient light intensity, humidity, heat); insect changes its rate of movement in relation to the stimulus intensity, but the direction of the movement is random.

Kineses are ***direct*** when the response is directly proportional to the stimulus intensity, ***inverse*** when inversely proportional to it.

A. Orthokinesis—*speed* of movement changes with stimulus intensity, including stopping and starting. [*e.g.* §7.3, p. 99; or *Tenebrio* moving slower in areas of low humidity.]

B. Klinokinesis—rate of *turning* changes with stimulus intensity. [*e.g.* §6.1.3, p. 82; or Human body louse turning more frequently near 30°C in a temperature gradient.]

II. Taxes—responses to *directional* stimuli (*e.g.* light rays, gravity, sound waves, scent trails, wind); the insect's movements are determined by the direction of the stimulus source; there are four principal types.

Taxes are ***positive*** when the movement is towards the stimulus source, ***negative*** when away from it.

A. Klinotaxis—stimulus sampled successively in time and space, classically by side-to-side head movements, but also including reverse turns on loss of a stimulus (esp. odour). [*e.g.* Blowfly larva moving away from a light.]

B. Tropotaxis—stimulus sampled continuously bilaterally; insect responds so as to keep this stimulation bilaterally balanced. When there are two sources of stimulation, insect bisects the angle to them as it moves. A bilateral pair of receptors is necessary, and the insect circles if one receptor is removed. [*e.g.* *Ephestia* caterpillar moving away from a light. Upwind orientation by a walking insect. §6.8.1, p. 94.]

C. Telotaxis—stimulus 'fixated' by anterior part of accurately directionally-sensitive receptor (esp. compound eye); bilateral input not necessary, one receptor will do. Insect moves straight to stimulus source (selecting one in preference if there is more than one). [*e.g.* Unilaterally blinded bee to a light. Tsetse fly to dark areas, p. 98.]

D. Menotaxis—stimulus 'fixated' as in telotaxis, but in any position; insect moves at a fixed angle to stimulus source. [*e.g.* Sun-compass orientation by ants and bees.]

Includes ***Optomotor responses***, in which apparent movement of the environment is corrected for [*e.g.* Station-keeping by pond-skaters in a stream.], or used [*e.g.* Upwind optomotor steering of flying male moths to female sex pheromone by the backward passage of the ground pattern on the retina, §6.8.1, p. 94.]

Kineses and taxes are also classified according to their relevant stimulus modalities: *photo-* (light), *chemo-* (odour, taste), *hygro-* (water), *mechano-* (motion, sound), *anemo-* (wind), *rheo-* (stream), *scoto-* (darkness), *phono-* (sound).

What happens is that odour stimulation switches on flight, which is then visually maintained in an upwind direction by the insect steering so that the ground pattern beneath it is kept moving backwards along its body axis. Any tendency to turn across the wind is detected as a change in this optomotor input, by the ground pattern tending to move transversely to the body axis.

Odour cues in the wind are fragmented because of air turbulence, so chemo-tactic steering in relation to odour gradients is probably not involved except perhaps very near the source. Although odour-evoked anemo-taxis in flying insects is therefore steered *visually,* the olfactory input is critical. A fall in odour concentration—e.g. because the insect has flown out of the odour 'plume'—causes the insect to turn and fly to-and-fro across the wind, thereby increasing its chances of finding the plume again. High concentration, on the other hand, causes the insect to slow down, land, and switch to direct visual orientation to the odour source. If the target is a mate, courtship and copulation then occur; if it is an animal or plant host, settling and feeding or oviposition occur.

6.8.2 Sensory cues in host finding

Whether the target is an animal or a plant, host finding invariably involves a sequence of responses to a sequence of different stimuli, as in the odour-evoked flight orientation just described (§6.8.1). At a distance, and especially at night, olfactory stimuli are important. For phytophagous insects, particular components of the plant's odour may be the most effective stimuli evoking orientation. For blood-sucking insects, it appears that the whole mixture of odours given off by the host is important; for although CO_2 by itself will evoke upwind flight, no other single component of vertebrate body odour has yet been found to do so.

   Closer to the host, and especially in daylight, visual stimuli become important. Thus, many phytophagous insects are attracted by the greenish-yellow hues of chlorophyll, and some respond specifically to the shapes of their host plants; some may even have optical interneurones which are pattern-specifically sensitive to the host plant's leaf shape. In winged aphids, dispersal to new host plants depends on a sequence of responses that starts with blue-photopositive flight up to the sky, and switches, after a few hours' carriage by the wind, to a green-yellow-positive descending flight that lands the aphid back on vegetation, well away from its overcrowded point of departure (see Fig. 6.2A). Diurnal blood-sucking insects like tsetse flies and tabanids, as well as responding to CO_2 and host odours, are activated by and attracted to large slowly moving visual targets such as men, cows, and even cars.

6.8.3 Host selection

This depends on three main factors: the ecological coincidence of insect and host; olfactory cues during the approach flight; and contact chemoreception (§4.5.1) once the insect has landed on the host. For phyto-phagous species, this last is particularly important—the migrating aphid starts immediately to probe when it lands on a new plant, and will take off again if not 'satisfied' (Fig. 6.2A). Rejection or acceptance of plant hosts often depends on the presence in their tissues of very small amounts of family- or genus-specific 'secondary plant substances' (i.e. non-nutritious compounds such as glucosides). For blood-sucking insects, on the other hand, such 'tasting' seems unimportant, since most species are prepared to feed on warmed fluids through artificial membranes (provided the fluid contains ATP), and discriminate little between different hosts when placed directly on their skin in the laboratory; presumably selection occurs earlier, at the anemotactic stage in the odour plume (§6.8.1).

Further reading

- Barton Browne L. (Ed.) (1974) *Experimental Analysis of Insect Behaviour.* Springer, Berlin, (For §6.1-6.8).
- Brady J. (1974) The physiology of insect circadian rhythms. *Adv. Insect Physiol.* **10**, 1-115 (For §6.3).
- Brady J. (1980) Behavioral rhythms in invertebrates. Chap. 8. In *The Handbook of Behavioral Neurobiology.* Vol. 4, *Biological Rhythms,* (Ed. J. Aschoff). Plenum, London. (For §6.3).
- Fraenkel G. S. & Gunn D. L. (1961) *The Orientation of Animals.* 2nd Edn. Dover, New York. (For §6.8).
- Huber F. (1978) The insect nervous system and insect behaviour. *Anim. Behav.* **26**, 969-981 (For §6.1).
- Manning A. (1979) *An Introduction to Animal Behaviour.* 3rd Edn. Arnold, London. (For §6.1, 6.2, 6.5, 6.7).
- Roeder K. D. (1967) *Nerve Cells and Insect Behaviour.* Harvard University Press, Cambridge, Mass. (For §6.1).
- Shorey H. H. *Animal Communication by Pheromones.* Academic Press, New York. (For §6.6).
- Truman J. W. & Riddiford L. M. (1974) Hormonal mechanisms underlying insect behaviour. *Adv. Insect Physiol.* **10**, 297-352 (For §6.4).
- Wilson E. O. (1971) *The Insect Societies.* Harvard University Press, Cambridge, Mass. (For §6.7).

Chapter 7
Interactions with the Environment

Three features of insects are of particular importance in determining their physiological relationship with the environment: their small size, their poikilothermy, and the impermeability and rigidity of their exoskeleton. Some of the consequences of these features are discussed in this last chapter, together with the physiology associated with the two most important temporal inputs from the environment—daily and seasonal periodicity.

7.1 THE PROBLEMS OF SMALL SIZE

The largest living insects, goliath beetles (*Goliathus goliathus*) are about 150 mm long and weigh over 40 g; the smallest, the egg-parasitic wasps (Mymaridae), are about 0.2 mm long and weigh less than half a microgram—a size range of at least 10^8. By comparison, flying birds range from around 15 Kg (swans, bustards) to 2 g (humming-birds)—a range of about 10^4. All birds and most insects fly by flapping their wings to generate aerodynamic *lift,* that is, an upward force at right angles to the direction of flight (p. 78). Insects less than about 1 mm long, however, can probably not do this. Their wings are too short to pass through the air fast enough to generate lift, because their speed is small relative to the density of the air (i.e. the Reynolds is very low) and the air thus becomes an effectively viscous medium for them. Under these circumstances, the insect can probably propel itself only by *drag*—using its wings as paddles, perhaps like the flippers of a frog-man.

Insects lose water and gain or lose heat through their surface cuticle (§2.5.1) and spiracles (§1.1.1). Since the surface area of a body is proportional to the square of its diameter, but its volume (and mass) varies as the cube of the diameter, the smaller the insect, the greater its surface:volume ratio (which increases in direct proportion to the decrease in the diameter). Hence a 5-mm long insect will have a surface:volume ratio about twice as great as that of a 10-mm long insect, and if its cuticle permeability is the same as the larger insect's, it will

lose water, or gain heat, etc., roughly twice as fast as the larger insect (such estimates can only be approximate, however, because of *allometry*—that is, a twice as 'big' insect will not normally have twice as long antennae, legs, etc.). Looked at another way, one can say that a small insect such as *Drosophila* (c. 3 mm long and 0.5 mg) is exposed to the environment through about 10 mm² of cuticle for each mg of body weight, whereas a larger, similarly shaped fly such as *Sarcophaga* (c. 15 mm long and 40 mg) is thus exposed via only about 2 mm² per mg (cf. a rat, via c. 0.1 mm² per mg).

Ecologically, on the other hand, the advantages of being small are manifold. Smallness permits the occupation of otherwise inaccessible niches (e.g. the Mymaridae—above) and the colonization of resources in vast numbers (see §7.3), with all the genetic and survival potentialities that that brings.

7.2 TEMPERATURE EFFECTS

The rate of all chemical reactions, and therefore most physiological processes, is dependent on temperature. The relationship is conveniently defined by the *temperature coefficient, Q_{10},* which is the ratio by which the rate of a given process increases for a 10°C increase in temperature. For physiological processes in insects, Q_{10}s of 2-3 are typical over the normal biological range (Fig. 7.1), that is, their rates approximately double for each 10° C rise. The main exceptions to this rule are biological clocks (§7.4, 7.5). In practice, Q_{10}s are not constant across the whole temperature range, however (Fig. 7.1). Being ratios, they are high at low temperatures, when physiological processes become very slow, and are low at high temperatures, falling to less than 1.0 near the upper lethal limit around 40°C, when enzyme inactivation sets in. Thus for the developmental rate of *Tenebrio* pupae, the Q_{10} is 6 at 10°, 3 at 20°, and 2 at 30° C.

Since insects are small and poorly insulated, their

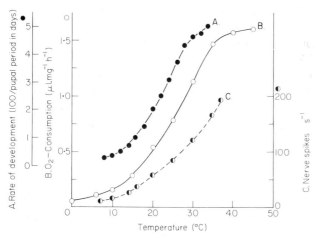

Fig. 7.1. Relationship between temperature and various physiological processes in insects. **A**, Rate of pupal development in the tsetse fly, *Glossina morsitans;* expressed as the reciprocal of the duration of the pupal period in days (After Phelps, R. J. & Burrows, P. M. (1969) *Entomologia exp. appl.* **12**, 33-44). **B**, Respiratory rate in 5-day-old pupae of the blowfly, *Phormia regina* (After Keister, M. & Buck, J. (1961) *J. Insect Physiol.* **7**, 51-72). **C**, Rate of spontaneous electrical activity in a nerve from the optic lobe of the blowfly, *Calliphora erythrocephala* (After Leutscher-Hazelhoff, J. T. & Kuiper, J. W. (1966) *The Functional Organization of the Compound Eye*, ed. C. G. Bernhard, pp. 483-492).

body temperature tends to be close to that of the environment (i.e. they are *poikilothermic*). They have, however, evolved many mechanisms to maintain themselves above low ambient temperatures. For example, in the bumble-bee (*Bombus affinis*), the enzyme F-1, 6-DP phosphatase has an unusually high activity—*c.* 40 × that in the honey-bee. This enables the bumble bee to generate heat by ATP hydrolysis (via the high activity of the substrate cycle between F-6-P and F-1, 6-DP—see §1.3), so that it can maintain a high thoracic temperature. As a result it can fly in substantially colder weather, and can forage much faster at low temperatures, than the honey-bee can. Many moths solve the same problem by fluttering their wings to warm up before they can fly; *Saturnia,* for example, can raise its thoracic temperature 10° C above an ambient of 18° by this means. Interestingly, both bumble-bees, which fly early in the year, and moths, which fly in the cold of night, are also partially insulated by cuticular 'fur'.

Since heat production in flight may exceed that at rest by a factor of 50, there is the converse problem in high ambient temperatures of overheating, especially for large insects. Thus prolonged flight in air temperatures above 38° C is impossible for locusts, because their thorax rapidly reaches a lethal 45° C. Flight in these circumstances is therefore interrupted by frequent periods of rest while the insect cools down. Butterflies probably solve this problem by gliding between brief bursts of flapping flight. Cooling can be effected by heat transfer in the haemolymph, sometimes by increased circulation from the thorax to the abdomen, and then mainly by evaporation of water via the spiracles (§1.1.1).

A prime adaptive value of behaviour is its use in maintaining homeostasis by orientational manoeuvres in relation to environmental conditions (§6.8), and behavioural adaptations to temperature are probably at least as important as biochemical ones. Thus on cold mornings, locusts 'bask' in the sun by standing at right angles to its rays and tilting their flanks to present the maximum surface for radiant heat absorption. At midday, however, they adopt the converse posture, hanging in the vegetation with their long axis parallel to the suns rays. The differential ratio of absorption is *c.* 6:1. Similarly, tsetse flies 'bask' in morning sunshine, but become strongly photo-negative when the air temperature rises above *c.* 32° C, when they fly to and remain in areas of deep shade.

For temperate zone insects, a major hazard lies in freezing in winter. If ice crystals form in the cells, delicate cellular structures may be damaged, and high, protein-denaturing salt concentrations may occur. These dangers are avoided in part by *supercooling* (in which the tissue fluids fall below 0° C without crystallizing—as will pure water in a capillary tube), in part by pre-winter concentration of the body fluids to lower their freezing point, and in part by the development of high levels of blood glycerol. This last probably acts both as an 'antifreeze' and as a buffer that ameliorates osmotic damage should crystals form. In this way the small parasitoid wasp, *Bracon cephi,* can withstand −47° C by carrying 5 M glycerol in its haemolymph, thereby lowering its freezing point by 17° C.

An important process in the development of such extreme low temperature tolerance is that the insect shall have had a period of several weeks' *acclimatization* to successively lower temperatures; sudden chilling of summer insects is usually fatal. In addition, the seasonal onset of diapause (§3.5) helps by redirecting the relevant metabolic pathways, and by changing behaviour so that dormancy is accompanied by avoidance reactions such as burrowing. Indeed, an obligatory minimum period at low temperature is usually required before diapause can be broken (§7.5).

7.3 MIGRATION

Many insects exploit temporary habitats (annual or patchy vegetation, ephemeral ponds, etc.) and have evolved migratory responses which permit them to escape from exhausted sites, usually by flight, and then to colonize fresh ones. To do this successfully, however, the migrant must arrive at the new site with a high reproductive potential. Migration thus tends to occur pre-reproductively, in newly-emerged adults, and forms a distinct phase in the life history, usually in the progeny of the generation directly affected by the deteriorated habitat.

Migratory behaviour is characterized by three features (see Kennedy, J. S. (1961) *Nature,* **189,** 785-791; Dingle, H. (1972) *Science, 175,* 1327-1335). (1) It involves heightened and prolonged locomotor activity (i.e. an increased orthokinesis—Table 6.1), so that the insect keeps moving for much longer than it does in normal 'trivial' flight within the habitat, generally for hours (aphids) or days (locusts) rather than for seconds or minutes. (2) This locomotor activity is relatively straightened out (i.e. it shows a decreased klinokinesis—Table 6.1), so that the flight takes the insect more rapidly away from its starting point. (3) It involves inhibition of those responses that the insect normally makes to stimuli from the habitat and which keep it there (food, resting sites, oviposition sites), with the inhibition being intense at the outset of a migratory flight but declining during it, until finally the insect will land again and reproduce in a new habitat.

Physiologically, migration is characterized by two prime features. It occurs in young, pre-reproductive adults, involving delayed reproductive development, with metabolism switched to increasing muscle growth and fat deposition at the expense of egg development. It is controlled, at least in part, by the same juvenile hormone (JH) system that regulates larval/adult and ovarian development (§3.3.5). In the migratory plant bug, *Oncopeltus,* the low post-metamorphic levels of JH in the blood are first replaced by intermediate titres which lead to migration (provided the daylength and temperature are appropriately spring-like). Then, some 10 days later, high JH titres are reached, reproduction is switched on, and non-migratory, settling behaviour is induced.

7.4 CIRCADIAN RHYTHMS

Insects, like all other animals, are typically *diurnal* (day active), *nocturnal* (night active) or *crepuscular* (dawn or dusk active). The timing of this *diel* (daily) rhythmicity is a species-specific characteristic due (a) to behavioural responses to daily changes in the environment (especially to temperature, humidity and light) and (b) to internal physiological timing.

A cockroach placed in an actograph (an apparatus for recording locomotor activity) and kept in a 12h light:12h dark cycle under constant conditions, performs the majority of its locomotor activity during the first hour or two of darkness every day (Fig. 7.2, days 1-10). This diel rhythm could be due either to a direct photokinetic response (Table 6.1) to the artificial sunset (i.e. be exogenously created), or to control from an internal physiological clock (i.e. be endogenously created). That the latter is the case is shown by placing the cockroach in constant darkness. Two central features of the rhythm are then revealed: (1) it continues indefinitely in the absence of environmental time-cues (light, temperature, noise, etc., all being held constant); (2) it drifts relative to external, solar time, occurring (in this animal) successively later and later (Fig. 7.2, days 10-20). The exact frequency of this *free-running* drift, as it is called, is a characteristic of the individual insect, whereas any uncontrolled potential environmental time-cues (barometric pressure, magnetic field, cosmic radiation, etc.) all occur with a precise 24-h periodicity (because they arise from the earth's rotation about its axis). Such rhythms must therefore be the result of endogenous timing from within the animal—i.e. be due to a physiological 'clock'.

Free-running drift away from solar time, when under constant conditions, is characteristic of all endogenously-

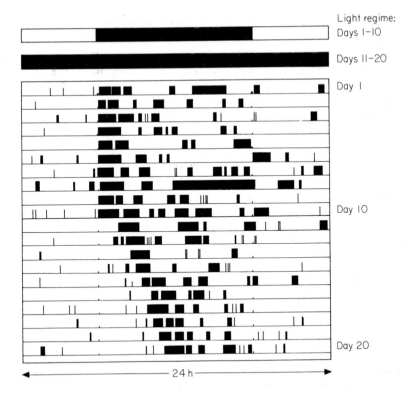

Fig. 7.2. Record of the locomotor activity of a cockroach kept for 20 days in a running-wheel actograph. Each horizontal line shows one day's record, with activity being indicated by the vertical marks; black blocks show particularly active periods where the vertical marks coalesce. Each day's record is presented in succession down the page. For the first 10 days the cockroach was in a 12 h light:12 h dark cycle; for the final 10 days it was in constant darkness. The light regime is indicated by the bars at the top of the figure.

timed daily rhythms, and is the origin of the term *circadian* used to describe them (from *circa diem,* about a day). The same principle applies to the other environmentally-related rhythms that occur in insects—tidal ('circa-tidal'), monthly ('circa-lunar') and annual ('circannual').

In nature, circadian rhythms do not normally free run, because conditions are never constant. The daily environmental changes *entrain* them to an exact 24-h periodicity, by causing a small daily *phase-shift* in the endogenous clock so that it is reset slightly each cycle by the necessary amount. In Fig. 7.2 this is implied by the difference between day 10 and day 11. Insect rhythms most commonly entrain to sunset or sunrise, but they will also entrain to temperature cycles, and in social insects to the activities of their colony mates (§6.7).

Circadian rhythms are, however, normally fairly stable, and resist large phase-shifts when subjected to experimentally applied changes in the environment. As a result, for example, it takes an insect several days before it adjusts to a reversed light cycle. Insect rhythms

can only be driven as fast as about 18 h or as slow as about 30 h per cycle. When attempts are made to drive a rhythm any faster, it skips alternate cycles and the insect is active every other experimental 'day'; when driven any slower it puts in two cycles to every one of the environment's.

A vital feature of this temporal stability of the underlying physiological clock is that although it will entrain to 24-h temperature *cycles* it is unaffected by the level of *constant* temperature. Were the clock to follow normal Q_{10} principles (§7.2), it could not keep time because it would run approximately twice as fast for every 10°C rise in temperature. In practice this does not occur, and circadian rhythms are *temperature-compensated,* with Q_{10}s of around unity. For example, the activity rhythm of the cockroach, *Periplaneta,* free runs with a period of 24.4 h at 19°C, and with a period of 25.8 h at 29°, a Q_{10} of 1.06. This independence of temperature is diagnostic of circadian rhythms (as well as of tidal, lunar, and annual rhythms), distinguishing them from virtually all other biological oscillations.

To summarize, circadian rhythms have three prime

characteristics: (1) they persist in the absence of external time-cues; (2) they persist at a period which is, in principle, never exactly 24 h but always close to it; (3) they are temperature-compensated, with Q_{10}s of *c.* 1.0.

The fact that locomotor activity is under circadian control reflects a much deeper temporal organization in insect physiology. Not only is much of behaviour controlled by a circadian clock (§6.3), but so also are nearly all other processes to a greater or lesser extent. This rhythmic organization extends into five general levels of organization (Table 7.1).

Table 7.1. EXAMPLES OF CIRCADIAN PHYSIOLOGI-CAL RHYTHMS IN INSECTS

1. **Cellular**—rhythms inherent in the metabolism of individual cells, e.g. in: *nuclear volume; RNA and protein synthesis; chitin secretion by epidermal cells.*
2. **Tissue**—rhythms occurring as a result of the synchronous activities of many cells in a tissue, e.g. in: *hormone secretion by brain neurosecretory cells and corpus allatum; cholinesterase activity in the CNS.*
3. **Whole Animal**—rhythms recognizable mainly as the physiological outcome of changes in the whole animal's metabolic state, e.g. in: *O_2-consumption; blood sugar levels; X-ray sensitivity.*
4. **Development**—once-in-a-lifetime events in growth and development detectable as rhythms only in populations, e.g. in: *hatching; pupation; eclosion.*
5. **Behaviour**—daily-repeated cycles of behaviour (cf. development) resulting from changes in CNS activity, e.g. in: *locomotor activity; feeding; oviposition; responsiveness to specific stimuli (see Fig. 6.5).*

It is not known how the biochemical oscillatory mechanism of any biological clock works, but something is known of how circadian clocks control some insect rhythms—that is, how the unseen underlying clock is coupled to the overt measurable rhythm it regulates. The eclosion rhythm of silk moths is the best understood example. The evidence runs as follows (see Truman J. W. & Riddiford L. M. (1970) *Science,* **167**, 1624-1626). (1) Intact moths in constant conditions emerge from the pupal case at a species-specific time of day—therefore eclosion is timed by a circadian rhythm. (2) If the pupal brain is removed, emergence occurs more or less normally, but at random times—therefore the brain is necessary only for the *timing* of eclosion, not for its motor co-ordination, which must be controlled by the ventral nerve cord. (3) Implantation of a brain into the abdominal haemocoel of brainless pupae restores their correct emergence timing, and injection of brain extracts from mature pupae into pupae due to emerge within a day or so induces them to emerge immediately—therefore the brain's control over emergence is by the circadian secretion of a pulse of hormone that releases eclosion behaviour.

It is not clear what roles hormones play in the control of other circadian rhythms in insects. It seems probable that all once-in-a-lifetime events (hatching, pupation, etc.) are, like eclosion, timed by hormones, and widespread cellular rhythms of the cuticle-deposition type (Table 7.1) may well be also; however, it is less likely that behaviour is. It was once thought (and is still claimed in some textbooks) that the activity rhythm of the cockroach is controlled by a hormone secreted from neurosecretory cells in the sub-oesophageal ganglion. This has now been shown to be most unlikely. It appears, instead, that a non-hormonal, direct neural coupling from the optic lobes of the brain is the crucial component, at least in the control of cockroach and cricket behavioural rhythms (see Brady J. (1969) *Nature, Lond.,* **223**, 781). Possibly the same kind of neural system controls the more complex aspects of the circadian organization of behaviour discussed in §6.3.

7.5 PHOTOPERIODISM AND DIAPAUSE

Most insects are affected by seasonal changes in the environment. Whether they have one generation a year (*univoltine*) or many (*multivoltine*), the onset of cold in winter or drought in summer has to be anticipated and its dangers avoided. Except near the equator, much the most reliable environmental cue as to the time of year is not temperature or rainfall, however, but daylength, and this is used by the great majority of species as a signal for developmental switching: into or out of diapause (§3.5 and below), change of polymorphic form (§3.3.6), or migration (§7.3).

This determination of physiological state by measurement of day-length is *photoperiodism*. It involves two processes: an internal physiological clock to measure the length of the day, and a mechanism for switching the developmental pathway when the clock gives the signal (§3.5). It is a quite different phenomenon from circadian, or annual rhythmicity (although it may be coupled to them, see below), because it involves a response to day *length* and is thus essentially environmentally determined, whereas a circadian or annual rhythm can, by definition, measure time (i.e. oscillate) *independently* of the environment (§7.4).

There is usually a *critical photoperiod* below which the physiological response occurs in only a few individuals, but above which the response occurs in most, or all of them. Either day-length or night-length may be measured, but in insects it is commonly the latter. Often the critical photoperiod is remarkably precise (Fig. 7.3 A): in the vetch aphid, *Megoura viciae*, a 15-min increase in night-length from 9 to 9¼ h switches some females from producing parthenogenetic offspring to producing sexually-reproducing offspring (§3.3.6), and an increase to 10 h causes the entire population to do so.

Because the relationship between season and day-length varies with latitude, the critical day-length for a particular response in a given species changes systematically in populations from different latitudes. The moth, *Acronycta rumicis,* for example, exists in several local races in Russia, each with a different critical day-length for diapause induction: 14½ h in the Black Sea race (43° N), 16½ h at Belgorod (50° N), 18 h at Vitebsk (55° N), and 19½ h at Leningrad (60° N). The earlier onset of winter in the north is thus allowed for by the earlier onset of diapause while the days are still relatively long.

The length of the critical photoperiod in insects is usually temperature-compensated, at least to some extent (§7.4). Other aspects of their photoperiodic responses may be greatly affected by temperature, however. Thus, critical day-length for diapause induction in pupae of the flesh-fly, *Sarcophaga argyrostoma,* is about 13½ h at all temperatures from 15° C to 25°,

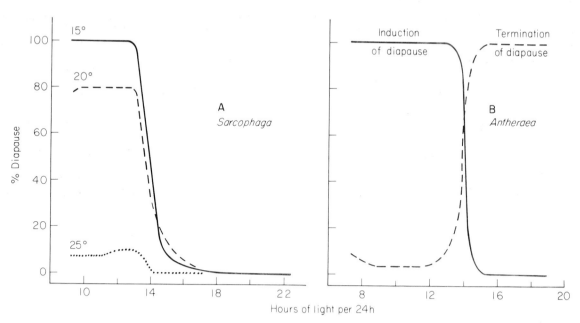

Fig. 7.3. Examples of photoperiodic diapause responses in insects. **A,** The induction of pupal diapause in the flesh-fly, *Sarcophaga argyrostoma,* at three temperatures, showing the sharp critical photoperiod of *c.* 13½ h of light per day; and that this critical day-length is unchanged over the temperature range 15-25°C, indicating good temperature-compensation (After Saunders, D. S. (1971) *J. Insect Physiol.* **17**, 801-812). **B,** The induction and termination of diapause in the silkmoth, *Antheraea pernyi,* showing that diapause is induced by the arrival in autumn of days shorter than *c.* 14 h, and that this diapause is broken by the arrival of spring days longer than *c.* 14 h; reciprocal critical photoperiods for induction and termination of diapause in this way are common in insects (After Williams, C. M. & Adkisson, P. L. (1964) *Biol. Bull.* **127**, 511-525).

but at 20° the maximum level of induction is only 80%, and at 25° very few larvae do diapause (Fig. 7.3 A). Evidently, although the photoperiodic clock is fully temperature-compensated, the physiological processes it controls can be uncoupled from it at ecologically unsuitable temperatures.

Two quite different kinds of photoperiodic timing mechanism occur in insects. In the first, the insect apparently measures the day—or night— length against its circadian periodicity, as if it were judging the time of sunrise and sunset by consulting its wrist-watch. In the second, the insect has an interval timer which starts at sunrise and stops at sunset (or *vice versa*) quite independently of any circadian rhythm, rather as if it were measuring critical day-length with an hourglass, by turning it over at sunrise and waiting to see if the sun set before or after the sand ran out. Circadian-based photoperiodic timing is involved in diapause induction in the flesh-fly (*Sarcophaga argyrostoma*) and the parasitic wasp (*Nasonia vitripennis*), hourglass-based timing in sexual polymorphism in the vetch aphid (*Megoura viciae*) and in larval diapause in the European corn borer (*Ostrinia nubilalis*).

Whichever kind of clock is used, several days and nights of the necessary length usually have to be experienced by the insect before physiological induction occurs. Parthenogenetic females of the vetch aphid, for example, must be exposed to some six cycles with short nights before they switch from producing sexual offspring to producing parthenogenetic offspring. This implies the gradual build up of an 'inductive state' until some threshold is reached (§3.3.6).

Once *diapause* has been photoperiodically induced it cannot be immediately broken by a return to favourable conditions: a minimum period in the dormant state must elapse first. This is what distinguishes diapause from mere *quiescence,* which can be broken at any time by placing the insect in favourable conditions. The relationship between diapause duration, and temperature, photoperiod (Fig. 7.3B), or water availability is complicated. The *termination of diapause* is often accelerated by some optimum temperature but delayed by either higher or lower temperatures. Thus, pupal diapause in the African moth, *Diparopsis castanea,* lasts 35 weeks at 22° C, drops to 25 weeks at its optimum of 28°, but rises again to 45 weeks at 37°. In temperate insects such optimum temperatures are usually adaptively related to the local mean winter temperature, commonly being a few degrees above freezing, e.g. 7° C for the termination of egg diapause in the silkmoth, *Bombyx mori* (§3.5).

Further reading

Brady J. (1974) The physiology of insect circadian rhythms. *Adv. Insect Physiol.,* **10**, 1-115 (For §7.4).

Brady J. (1979) *Biological Clocks;* Studies in Biology No. 104; Arnold, London (For §7.4, 7.5).

Hardy R. N. (1972) *Temperature and Animal Life;* Studies in Biology No. 35; Arnold, London (For §7.2).

Johnson C. G. (1969) *Migration and Dispersal of Insects by Flight;* Methuen, London (For §7.3).

Lees A. D. (1955) *The Physiology of Diapause in Arthropods;* Cambridge University Press, London (For §7.5).

Saunders D. S. (1976) *Insect Clocks;* Pergamon, London (For §7.4, 7.5).

Wigglesworth V. B. (1972) *The Principles of Insect Physiology,* 7th Edn, chap. 15; Chapman & Hall, London (For §7.2).

Index